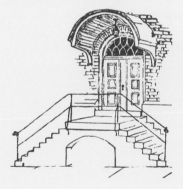

UNDERSTANDING
LILLIAN HELLMAN

Understanding Contemporary American Literature
Matthew J. Bruccoli, Series Editor

Volumes on

Edward Albee • Nicholson Baker • John Barth
Donald Barthelme • The Beats • The Black Mountain Poets
Robert Bly • Raymond Carver • Chicano Literature
Contemporary American Drama
Contemporary American Horror Fiction
Contemporary American Literary Theory
Contemporary American Science Fiction
James Dickey • E. L. Doctorow • John Gardner • George Garrett
John Hawkes • Joseph Heller • Lillian Hellman • John Irving
Randall Jarrell • William Kennedy • Ursula K. Le Guin
Denise Levertov • Bernard Malamud • Carson McCullers
W. S. Merwin • Arthur Miller • Toni Morrison's Fiction
Vladimir Nabokov • Gloria Naylor • Joyce Carol Oates
Tim O'Brien • Flannery O'Connor • Cynthia Ozick • Walker Percy
Katherine Anne Porter • Reynolds Price • Thomas Pynchon
Theodore Roethke • Philip Roth • Hubert Selby Jr. • Mary Lee Settle
Isaac Bashevis Singer • Jane Smiley • Gary Snyder
William Stafford • Anne Tyler • Kurt Vonnegut
Tennessee Williams • August Wilson

UNDERSTANDING
LILLIAN
HELLMAN

Alice Griffin and Geraldine Thorsten

University of South Carolina Press

© 1999 University of South Carolina

Published in Columbia, South Carolina, by the
University of South Carolina Press

Manufactured in the United States of America

03 02 01 00 99   5 4 3 2 1

Library of Congress Cataloging-in-Publication Data

Griffin, Alice, 1924–
   Understanding Lillian Hellman / Alice Griffin and Geraldine
Thorsten
      p. cm. — (Understanding contemporary American literature)
   Includes bibliographical references (p.) and index.
   ISBN 1-57003-302-1
   1. Hellman, Lillian, 1906- —Criticism and interpretation.
2. Women and literature—United States—History—20th century.
I. Thorsten, Geraldine. II. Title. III. Series.
PS3515.E343 Z69 1999
812'.52—ddc21   98-58042

To John A. and John B.

To my mother, Tressie Williams,
and my beloved family and friends

CONTENTS

Editor's Preface   ix

Preface   xi

Acknowledgments   xv

Abbreviations   xvii

   Chapter 1   Career   1

   Chapter 2   *The Children's Hour*   27

   Chapter 3   *Another Part of the Forest* and
               The Little Foxes   39

   Chapter 4   *Watch on the Rhine*   63

   Chapter 5   *The Autumn Garden*   76

   Chapter 6   *Toys in the Attic*   89

   Chapter 7   *An Unfinished Woman* and *Pentimento*   100

   Chapter 8   *Scoundrel Time*   119

   Chapter 9   *Maybe*   127

Notes   135

Bibliography   147

Index   159

EDITOR'S PREFACE

The volumes of the Understanding Contemporary American Literature (UCAL) series have been planned as guides or companions for students as well as nonacademic readers. The editor and publisher perceive a need for these volumes because much influential contemporary literature makes special demands. Uninitiated readers encounter difficulty in approaching works that depart from the traditional forms and techniques of prose and poetry. Literature relies on conventions, but the conventions keep evolving; new writers form their own conventions—which in time may become familiar. Put simply, UCAL provides instruction in how to read certain contemporary writers—identifying and explicating their material, themes, use of language, point of view, structures, symbolism, and responses to experience.

The word *understanding* in the titles was deliberately chosen. Many willing readers lack an adequate understanding of how contemporary literature works; that is, what the author is attempting to express and the means by which it is conveyed. Although the criticism and analysis in the series have been aimed at a level of general accessibility, these introductory volumes are meant to be applied in conjunction with the works they cover. They do not provide a substitute for the works and authors they introduce, but rather prepare the reader for more profitable literary experiences.

M. J. B.

PREFACE

As a child perched in a tree Lillian Hellman spied her father paying court to another woman. Angered at the injustice to her mother, the youngster fell from the tree and broke her nose, an early display of the dramatic expression of morality that would mark her life and works. Whether the injustice was "the big lie" that destroys the lives of two women in *The Children's Hour,* the exploitation of the South in *The Little Foxes,* or the wholesale savaging by the House Un-American Activities Committee in *Scoundrel Time,* Hellman was never reluctant to fight against what she saw as wrongs.

She learned as a teenager that "If you are willing to take the punishment, you are halfway through the battle," and she accepted the punishments along with the rewards in her life. She began her theater career in the thirties, when women playwrights were pronounced inferior to male playwrights by the "dean" of drama critics, George Jean Nathan. Most of the critics, who were male, did not accord her works any in-depth analysis and dismissed them as melodramas. Not until recently was she recognized as an influence on other major playwrights such as Tennessee Williams and Arthur Miller and as a "beacon of hope" to a younger generation of women playwrights like Marsha Norman.

On the occasion of her fall, the child accepted her nurse's caution—"Don't go through life making trouble for people"—but thereafter Hellman would ignore this good advice. When friends advised her not to write *Scoundrel Time,* her experiences with and opinions about the McCarthy era, she went ahead and did so. The book, published in 1976, has been described as a storm center that created a flood of adverse criticism, not only from long-standing enemies alienated by her frank opinions and/or espousal of liberal causes but also from her former allies among the liberals, whom the book attacks for their inaction in the face of injustice. Her satire is biting, as might be expected from one devoted to Voltaire and his attacks on "all human nonsense." (She wrote the book for Leonard Bernstein's musical version of *Candide,* a work he undertook at her suggestion.)

The one person whose advice she did accept was Dashiell Hammett, with whom she lived for thirty years, beginning with their meeting when she was twenty-four and the tall, thin detective-fiction writer was thirty-six. After his death in 1961, she was asked to edit an anthology of his short stories, and the introduction she wrote about him helped persuade her to embark on a memoir, *An Unfinished Woman* (1969), which concludes with the Hammett profile. Four more memoirs followed, her prose style notable not only for the precision and clarity that marked her dramas but also for its use of such poetic devices as free association, elliptical time, and symbolism.

Hellman's refusal to live within the narrow limits deemed acceptable for women of her generation made her personal life a subject of interest greater than the attention paid to her art. People were fascinated by her love affairs, her relationship with Hammett (whom she never married but allowed her moralistic mother to assume she had), her visits to Spain during its civil war and the Russian front in World War II, and her refusal to "name names" in the McCarthy era.

PREFACE

Since Hellman's death in 1984 there have been biographies favorable and unfavorable, and at least three plays about her life, but no volume of in-depth critical evaluation of her works has appeared since the 1979 publication (before *Three* and *Maybe* were published) of Katherine Lederer's analytical *Lillian Hellman*, which concentrates on the dramas. We hope our book will fill the need created by the steadily growing resurgence of interest in Lillian Hellman's literary works and that our assessments will enable viewers and readers to more deeply appreciate and enjoy her remarkable contributions to contemporary American literature. In keeping with the editorial goals of this series, the major dramas and all the memoirs are discussed in depth, with analyses of characters, plot, themes, theatrical and literary effects, and language. Each work is considered as an artistic entity, to which a chapter or half chapter is devoted.

ACKNOWLEDGMENTS

We appreciate the helpful advice and assistance from friends and colleagues, including Rosalee Abrams, Constance Anestis, Jeri Butler, Julie Bowdler, Margot Mink Colbert, Edith Conn, Jean DeCock, Ruth Goldman, and Susan Voge. We also wish to thank Peter Feibleman and Rita Wade. Our work was greatly facilitated by the generous assistance of the staffs of the British Library; the Library of Lehman College of the City University of New York; the Martin County, Florida, Library System; and the New York Public Library for the Performing Arts. We extend particular thanks to librarians Muriel Knobloch of Lehman College, Jay Barksdale and Vivian Gonzalez of the New York Public Library, and curator Marty Jacobs of the Theater Collection of the Museum of the City of New York.

Our greatest debt of gratitude goes to our families for their unfailing encouragement and support, and to them, with love and thanks, this volume is dedicated.

ABBREVIATIONS

Because of the various editions available, quotations from the plays (taken from *The Collected Plays*) are referred to in the text by act and/or scene instead of by page numbers. Quotations in the text from the memoirs are referred to by page numbers of the original individual editions. References to the memoirs in chapters other than those devoted to a particular memoir are designated as follows:

UW *An Unfinished Woman*
P   *Pentimento*
ST   *Scoundrel Time*
T   *Three*
M   *Maybe*

UNDERSTANDING
LILLIAN HELLMAN

CHAPTER ONE

Career

Lillian Florence Hellman was born in New Orleans on 20 June 1905, the only child of Julia Newhouse Hellman and Max Hellman, whose family had emigrated from Germany in the 1840s. *An Unfinished Woman* depicts her father as stern yet loving and her mother as gentle, devout, and highly moral. An only child, Hellman acknowledges that "I was off balance in a world where I knew my grand importance to two other people who certainly loved me for myself, but who also liked to use me against each other" (UW 8).

When her father's shoe business failed and he became a traveling salesman, six-year-old Lillian and her mother then spent six months each year in New Orleans with her father's unmarried sisters in their boardinghouse. They also spent six months in New York with the Newhouses. "I made my New Orleans teachers uncomfortable because I was too far ahead of my schoolmates, and my New York teachers irritable because I was too far behind" (UW 10). John Hersey reports, "There was a year of sharp turn toward rebelliousness in her, when she was 13 or 14,"[1] a trait common among maturing young women, who often will rebel against a disliked status quo.

After attending Wadleigh High School in New York, Lillian entered New York University. "I was overproud, oversensitive, overdaring because I was shy and frightened," she writes. Leaving college in her junior year, she found work with the distinguished publishing firm of Horace Liveright, where she soon feared she would be fired: "I didn't know how to file, my typing was erratic, and my manuscript reports were severe" (UW 31, 38). Instead, she left to marry theater press agent Arthur Kober. She was twenty. She reflects that she was bewildered and impatient, "certain only that any adventure was worth having, and increasingly muddled by the Puritan conscience that made me pay for the adventures" (UW 53).

In Paris with Kober, who had been offered a magazine job there, Hellman wrote and published short stories, "lady writer" stuff.[2] She then worked as a press agent, a play reader, and, in Rochester, New York, as a theater publicist, winning enough money from gambling to travel in 1929 to Bonn, Germany, where she decided to study at the university. Waiting to enroll, she was invited by students to join their organization, "no dues for foreigners if they had no Jewish connections." She informed them that, except for a distant in-law, all in her family were Jewish. The next day she left for New York (UW 54).

During the depression Kober was gaining a reputation as a writer of short stories for *The New Yorker* and the comedy *Having Wonderful Time*. He was offered a job as a scenario writer in Hollywood, where Hellman found work reading manuscripts for Metro-Goldwyn-Mayer. The stuffy workroom was dispiriting; she would linger late to avoid the ride to their dark, rented house: "I did not yet know about 'inhuman cities' or roads built with no relief for the eye, or the effects of a hated house upon the spirit. I didn't even understand about my marriage, or my life" (UW 60).

Longing for a "cool teacher," Hellman met Dashiell Hammett in a restaurant in Hollywood when she was twenty-four and he was thirty-six, recovering from "a five-day drunk." They talked about the poems of T. S. Eliot in Hammett's car until daylight, met again a few weeks later, "and, after that, on and sometimes off again for the rest of his life and thirty years of mine" (UW 259). "I had found somebody who stood by himself, who was himself. For many people that would not be much to find: for me, even when I disagreed, it came at a time when I was going under" (T 304). In 1934 she and Arthur Kober were divorced.

Tall, thin, and handsome, Hammett, a former Pinkerton detective, was a famous writer of detective stories, including *The Glass Key* and *The Maltese Falcon.* In 1933 *The Thin Man* introduced a new breed of hero-sleuth: Nick Charles, suave, sophisticated, and witty, an alter ego of Hammett himself. Wife Nora, based on Hellman, to whom the novel is dedicated, is another "first" for the genre—an equal partner, whether drinking, suggesting solutions, or exchanging racy remarks. The success of the book was repeated in the *Thin Man* movie series, starring William Powell as Nick, and Myrna Loy as Nora. "Some of the dialogue is almost direct quotation from me, but she is Hammett's picture of me. I don't see myself," remarked Hellman. "It's an affectionate portrait of a woman; but what pleased me more than anything else was that it was an affectionate pair of people. A man and woman who amused each other and got along."[3] Their relationship, in its best moments, was marked by the wit, sexiness, and sophistication personified by Nick and Nora. In its worst moments there were quarrels, Hammett's alcoholism (as well as her own), his womanizing, and his syphilis.

When Hellman decided to write a drama, it was Hammett who suggested that a beginning writer should work within an established framework. He referred her to *Bad Companions* by Scottish law historian William Roughead, whose books documented interesting trials. The chapter "Closed Doors" details a lawsuit in Edinburgh in the early nineteenth century: fourteen-year-old Anglo-Indian Jane, enrolled in a genteel boarding school run by two ladies in their late twenties, accuses the teachers of lesbianism, or, in Roughead's words, "inordinate affection for one another." Their lawsuit for defamation of character, and subsequent appeals that lasted ten years, cost them the school and ruined their lives.[4] After six drafts, Hellman's play, under Hammett's tutelage, emerged as *The Children's Hour.*

The Children's Hour is a remarkable achievement, especially for a first play. Sharp, economical dialogue develops the main characters, and the plotting is taut, as the accusing student's "big lie" reaps disastrous effects. Although the producer worried that the play would be banned, *The Children's Hour* was an instant hit when it opened on Broadway in December 1934. This was largely due to Hellman's skill in focusing on sympathetic characters rather than a sensational subject. She was twenty-nine. The play ran for 691 performances and toured the United States. "I don't think success or failure meant much to me then," she recalled years later, "and when success came, I gave it four days of fun and then ran away fast, frightened that it would become a way of life."[5]

Within a month of the opening Hellman went to Hollywood, engaged to write the screen version, *These Three,* as well as other films. *These Three,* where the charge is infidelity, not lesbianism, was an artistic and popular success. The play was revived on Broadway in the fifties, and a 1962 movie used the original plot and title.

In the fall of 1937, en route to a theater festival in Moscow, Hellman was in Paris. Friends there urged her to go to Spain, then embroiled in a civil war between the Loyalists, supporters of the republic, and the Fascists, headed by future dictator Francisco Franco. In *An Unfinished Woman* she writes of her Spanish experiences in the form of a diary, parts of which were published in 1938 and 1942.[6] Hellman feared that the Spanish conflict was the prelude to a second world war.

When she was invited to the theater festival, Hammett predicted she would not enjoy it: "You don't like the theatre except the times when you're in a room by yourself putting the play on paper." Hellman confesses that the world of the theater "is not my world, although it has been my life" (UW 75). "The theater," she commented, "is a world of fashion, and fashions turn, and I guess you just pray you'll live long enough to see them turn back again. Your job is to pay no attention to them."[7]

She reports in *Pentimento* the disastrous opening night of her second play, *Days to Come,* on 15 December 1936 and her feelings of guilt for its failure (P 161–62). Her participation in the Hollywood struggle to create a union for screenwriters may have suggested the play's subject: the conflict between labor and management. Neither side wins. Rodman, a paternalistic factory owner, fails to act decisively when a strike is threatened, and his inaction precipitates disaster. Strike breakers are called in and their criminal tactics lead to murder. Rodman's unfaithful wife, attracted to the falsely accused labor organizer, clears his name by compromising her own.

"It's the family I'm interested in principally," said Hellman. "The strike and social manifestations are just backgrounds. It's a story of innocent people on both sides who are drawn into conflict and events far beyond their comprehension. It's the saga of a man who started something he cannot stop, a parallel among adults to what I did with children in *The Children's Hour*."[8]

Thirty-five years later, Hellman reflected about *Days to Come:* "It is crowded and over-wrought, but it is a good report of rich liberals in the 1930s, of a labor leader who saw through them, of a modern lost lady, and has in it a correct prediction of how conservative the American labor movement was to become" (P 163).

The play's closing after seven performances may have prompted the care Hellman took with her next work, *The Little Foxes,* rewriting it eight times. Hellman gathered extensive notes on the period of 1880–1900 in the South, everything from the political situation to gardening, food, and decoration. Her principal characters reflect her mother's wealthy, materialistic family, whose Sunday dinners had their humorous side, but there young Lillian also became aware of the "injustice of socially ordained inferiority visited especially on blacks and on women."[9] In the drama the Hubbards, terrifying but also comic in their greed and acquisitiveness, achieve power and wealth by exploiting the less fortunate. Regina and her brothers, Ben and Oscar, engage in a power struggle to control even more wealth by bringing cotton mills to the South. Hellman was surprised when reviewers depicted Regina as a villain: "I just meant her as a cold lady, I didn't mean her as bad, particularly. I was very shocked when everybody said she was [bad]."[10]

Opening on Broadway in 1939 the play was an instant success (as was the motion picture, scripted by Hellman), though she was disappointed with the reviewers, who saw the characters as types and the plot as melodramatic. One critic who dismissed it as "febrile," Hellman recalls, later termed it "an American classic without explaining why he changed his mind" (P 179). *The Little Foxes* earned the playwright enough money to buy a 130–acre farm in Westchester County, New York, where she and Hammett were to live for thirteen pleasant years, during which she wrote her best plays, including *Watch on the Rhine* and *The Autumn Garden.*

Watch on the Rhine, Hellman recalls, was inspired by Henry James's novels *The American* and *The Europeans:* "I wanted to write a play about nice, liberal Americans whose lives would be shaken up by Europeans, by a world the new Fascists had won because the old values had been long dead" (P 186). Although the play opened in early 1941, by December of that year and Pearl Harbor it was even more timely. A wealthy, liberal widow and her son welcome to their suburban Washington home her son-in-law, a German anti-Fascist who had fought in Spain. Kurt, dedicated to the cause of freedom, is contrasted to a Rumanian houseguest, who attempts to betray Kurt to the Nazis. Brooks Atkinson of the *New York Times* commented, "The play has grace and humor—witty dialogue, a tender feeling for the children, respect for character, and an undertone of good-natured family banter."[11]

In early 1944 *The Searching Wind* again treated American complacency and compromise with the enemies of freedom. A love triangle is played out during four historical periods: Washington in 1944, with diplomat Alexander Hazen at home with his wife and son; in flashbacks, Rome in 1922, when Mussolini takes over; Berlin in 1923, when the Fascists attempt to assume power; and Paris in 1938, just before the Munich conference. Robert P. Newman sees Hazen, who is as indecisive in political situations as he is in his emotional relationships, as Hellman's view of diplomats: "a wimp, refusing to take a stand against fascism."[12] The work had a moderate success as a play and as a movie written by Hellman.

Hellman's third work concerning World War II was a screenplay, *The North Star.* Originally intended as a semidocumentary to be made in Russia, it was encouraged by the Roosevelt administration in order to counter Americans' anti-Russian feelings stemming from Russia's earlier alliance with Nazi Germany. (The Soviet Union was a U. S. ally by the time of the movie.) When it was decided to film in Hollywood, Samuel Goldwyn hired Aaron Copland to write music and Ira Gershwin to write lyrics for what evolved not as a serious motion picture but a "semi-musical," with four musical numbers, "all of them pedestrian."[13] "It could have been a good picture instead of the big-time, sentimental, badly directed, badly acted mess it turned out to be," says Hellman (UW 125). Enraged, she bought back her contract from Goldwyn and published her original screenplay when the altered film was released in 1943. The North Star is a commune from which four young people set out for a hiking holiday; that day, Germany attacks Russia. While Hellman visualizes cinematically the devastating effects of the invasion on the village, her best scene is the confrontation between the Russian doctor (Walter Huston) and the Nazi doctor (Erich von Stroheim), whose staff is drawing blood from local children for transfusions for German soldiers.

In 1944, Hellman writes in *Pentimento,* she was invited on a cultural mission by the Russians as two of her plays were being rehearsed in Moscow, *The Little Foxes* and *Watch on the Rhine.* The Roosevelt administration encouraged her acceptance. While in Moscow she met John Melby, a young diplomat at the American embassy. Their affair developed into a serious love relationship, one that would later, in the McCarthy era, cost Melby his career.[14]

When World War II was over, Hellman turned to the trilogy in which she had intended *The Little Foxes* to occupy the central position. Instead of carrying the time forward, the writer chose to delineate the younger Hubbards twenty years earlier, seeing analogies between the post–Civil War era and the then-current postwar period. In *Another Part of the Forest* family tyrant Marcus has profited during the war by shady dealings; son Ben is as anxious as his father is reluctant to invest in the nation's expanding economy; and daughter Regina aims at independence by indulging their father. Mother Lavinia is dismissed by Marcus as ineffectual until power shifts to Ben.

Hellman attempts to satirize the "wild and funny" goings-on she remembered from Sunday dinners with the large "banking, storekeeping" Newhouse family, and the "high-spirited talk and laughter from the older people of who did what to whom . . . [and] what benefits the year had brought from the Southern business interests they had left behind for the Northern profits they had had sense enough to move toward" (P 180, 182). Although the play was well received by audiences, the reviewers saw only melodrama and missed the satire.

In 1949 Hellman adapted the French play *Montserrat,* by Emmanuel Roblès, about an officer in the Spanish army of occupation in Venezuela who sympathizes with Simon Bolivar, leader of the revolution in 1812. Central to the play is the debate between cynical Spanish officer Izquierdo and Montserrat, who will not divulge Bolivar's whereabouts even though it costs the lives of innocent hostages. The play, which opened 29 October 1949, was criticized by the reviewers as verbose and unfocused. Harold Clurman in *The New Republic* (5 December 1949) saw the work as existential, dealing with choice: Montserrat must choose whether the good of millions outweighs the death of a few; having made his choice, he must bear responsibility for the outcome.

Seeking calm when hard at work, Hellman writes: "long days, months of fiddling is the best way of life. I wrote *The Autumn Garden* in such a period. I was at a good age; I lived on a farm that was, finally, running fine and I knew I had found the right place to live for the rest of my life." She and Hammett had been together almost twenty years: "Without words, we knew that we had survived for the best of all reasons, the pleasure of each other" (P 199).

The Autumn Garden, Hellman believes, is her best play. With dramatic skill and mature insight, she depicts seven middle-aged people in the autumn of their lives, who meet again after two decades to reevaluate the past and to realize that they have been shaped by choices made over the years. There is little action except in the final scene, where there may be too much action. Outstanding for its revelation of character, the play opened in March 1951 to respectful reviews and a not overlong run of 102 performances. Brooks Atkinson of the *New York Times* found it "boneless and torpid" (8 March 1951), but its reputation has grown steadily since.

Later that year Hammett was sentenced to prison by the House Un-American Activities Committee (HUAC) for refusing to disclose names of donors to a bail fund. Hellman reports that Hammett did not know the names, but declined to answer as a matter of principle. By the time he was released from jail, the farm had been sold to pay legal expenses and back taxes for Hammett, whose present and future royalties were impounded. Even more difficulties were to follow.

Hellman was summoned to appear before HUAC in May 1952. *Scoundrel Time* (1976) chronicles her appearance on May 21, and the weeks leading to it. In a letter of May 19 to the committee, she offered to answer any questions about herself, but she would not "name names," a committee requisite. She stated that she could not "hurt innocent people whom I knew many years ago in order to save myself." The committee rejected her offer, but at the hearing, once her letter was read into the record, it could be distributed to a full press gallery. Knowing they were in a difficult position, the committee dismissed Hellman.

Although she won a moral victory, times would be hard in the ensuing years, for she was blacklisted and could not earn a livelihood by writing. By then, Hammett, a heavy smoker who had chronic bronchitis, was ill with emphysema. At one point Hellman took a job selling groceries at Macy's under an assumed name.[15] Then Louis Kronenberger, an editor and theater critic, asked her to edit Chekhov's *Selected Letters.* Hellman's introduction to the volume, published in 1955, appreciates those qualities in Chekhov like her own: "toughness of mind and spirit" and his "contempt for self-deception and hypocrisy." She could sympathize when his plays were misinterpreted: *The Cherry Orchard* and *The Sea Gull* should have been presented as comedies, not tragedies, as staged by Stanislavsky.[16]

Two adaptations from the French were to follow. She adapted Jean Anouilh's *The Lark,* "convinced that Joan was history's first modern career girl, wise, unattractive in what she knew about the handling of men, straight out of a woman's magazine" (P 202). Dramatically, Hellman's version, which opened 17 November 1955, is an improvement on Anouilh, who treats the English occupation of France during Joan's time in terms of the Nazi occupation during World War II. Discursive political and philosophical passages, pitting man against ideology, were cut by Hellman, who tightened the plot, added mime and pageantry to carry the action forward, and fashioned hardhitting, economical dialogue. Hellman's theme is that "man's courage, as characterized by Joan, will prevail despite efforts to destroy it."[17]

Hellman's next adaptation was Voltaire's *Candide* as the book for a musical by Leonard Bernstein. She had suggested the venture to Bernstein in 1950, but they did not begin work on it until six years later.[18] Her libretto (in *Collected Plays*) is praised by Gerald Weales for setting up "the situations in which the musical numbers can do their satirical work," and for contributing "to the satirical effect of the operetta as a whole. She manages to do what most musical adaptations never even attempt to do, retain the artistic intention of the original work in the new form." The tone, notes Weales, matches Voltaire's satire, and the result is "the most sophisticated product of the American musical stage." But Weales believes that the musical's transition is too abrupt from its "brittle tone" to its concluding moments, a "hymnlike finale."[19] Brooks Atkinson of the *New York Times* judged both text and score of *Candide* to be "distinguished"; yet "despite its artistic expertness and cultural value, it failed."[20] Because the production, which opened 1 December 1956, required Hellman's collaboration not only with Bernstein but with lyricists, producers, the director, and the designer, her original book was considerably altered: "I took suggestions and made changes that I didn't believe in, tried making them with speed I cannot manage" (P 203).

Complaining two years later to Edmund Wilson about her writing block, Hellman was told, "A writer writes. That's all there is to it." The next day, she went to work on *Toys in the Attic,* which opened in February 1960. Considered by many to be Hellman's finest play, it won the Drama Critics' Circle Award.

To the reviewers who charged that *Toys in the Attic* drew its inspiration from the plays of Tennessee Williams, Jacob Adler replied, "People who see signs in the New Orleans setting and in some of the play's gaudier details that Miss Hellman was capitalizing on Williams apparently forget that Miss Hellman has never hesitated to call a spade by its most accurate name, or to look into any cranny of life which pertains to her dramatic idea."[21] Charlotte Goodman points out that the influence actually worked the other way around: "Her creation of various speech patterns to differentiate her characters, and her pungent blend of humor, pathos, and irony are also found in Williams's plays. When one considers that Hellman was the first American playwright to make productive use of the mores of the changing South in the theater, it is ironic that some reviewers accused Hellman of imitating Williams." Goodman also notes "the relevance of her work to that of younger American dramatists such as Miller and Williams."[22]

Toys in the Attic was an immediate success when it opened in February 1960. "The money came at the right time," writes Hellman, "because for a year I had known that death was on Hammett's face and I had worried abut how we could manage what I thought would be the long last days" (P 208). He died of lung cancer less than a year later.

My Mother, My Father, and Me, Hellman's adaptation of Burt Blechman's novel *How Much?,* is a farcical satire of the generation gap, involving spendthrift mother, worried father, hippie son, outspoken black cook, and indulgent grandmother. It opened 21 March 1963 and closed after a brief run. Hellman attributes its failure not only to poor production and direction: "I found that I had made some of the same mistakes I had made with *Candide:* I changed the tone midway from farce to drama and that, for reasons I still do not understand, cannot be done in the theatre" (P 209).

Meanwhile, recognition for Hellman's literary achievement was growing. Brandeis University bestowed on her their
Creative Arts Medal in 1961, and the National Institute of Arts
and Letters awarded her the Gold Medal for drama in 1964. She
taught writing at Hunter College as well as at Harvard, Yale,
M.I.T., and the University of California at Berkeley. *My
Mother, My Father, and Me* was the last play Lillian Hellman
would write, but it was not the end of Lillian Hellman as a
writer.

In 1969 *An Unfinished Woman* was published and won the
National Book Award. It was the first of her four memoirs,
which set a new style for autobiography by using elliptical time
and free association. Sometimes within a single sentence time
moves from past to near past to present to past. Other innovations included a cinematic fading or dissolving from one incident to another, poetic symbolism, and surrealistic details.
Pentimento followed in 1973; *Scoundrel Time* in 1976; *Three,*
a collection of the memoirs with added commentary, in 1979;
and *Maybe* in 1980. Richard Poirier believes that in the memoirs Hellman "works against her own tendencies to be
assertive, stabilized, moralistic, and knowing." In her "prose
portraiture and reminiscence," he observes, "the writing . . .
does not so much communicate her already confirmed sense of
a place or a person; rather it enacts her own quite tentative
explorations of them." She questions "the motives, even the
authenticity of what was written the moment before." He notes
that "an event, bathed in the atmosphere of her style, is, as in a
dream, indivisibly the source of radiating impressions and
experiences."[23]

As the memoirs appeared, Hellman received additional awards, as well as honorary degrees, from Columbia, Yale, Tufts, and Rutgers universities. In those same years the growing women's movement would recognize in Hellman the qualities they espoused—"independence, outspokenness, intense moralism—her refusal to conform, above all."[24] She took a commonsense approach to the movement, insisting that women's major concern should be economic equality: "It all comes down to whether or not you can support yourself as well as a man can support himself and whether there's enough money to make certain decisions for yourself rather than dependence." "The big battle is equal rights . . . . Nobody can argue any longer about the rights of women. It's like arguing about earthquakes."[25]

Independence to Hellman did not mean sacrificing her femininity. She loved fashionable clothes and good accessories, and wore them with style, as her photographs indicate. Believing it was important to present herself visually in the best possible light, she reports that the Balmain dress she wore for her appearance before the HUAC made her "feel better." "Genuinely feminine" is Margaret Case Harriman's description of Hellman in a 1941 *New Yorker* profile.[26]

The attention she received with the publication of the memoirs was a far cry from the early days of her career, when her status as a playwright who happened to be a woman meant that plays like *The Children's Hour* received scant, often dismissive, critical attention. George Jean Nathan, the "dean" of theater critics, summed up the earlier attitude: "Even the best of our women playwrights [Hellman] falls considerably short of the mark of our best masculine." Major reviewers—all of them male—followed Nathan's lead in declaring Hellman's first plays to be melodramas, attributed, says Nathan, to a "generic feminine inability or perhaps disinclination to hold the emotions within bounds." He believes "it is apparently very difficult for a woman playwright to see her leading characters with a complete objectivity," and declares, "I can at the moment recall no play pretending to quality written by an American woman in the last dozen years whose central characters have not at one point or another suffered critically from the personal sympathy or personal dislike of their author." Nathan does, however, admit of Hellman that "if she has the dramatic faults inherent in her gender, she also has virtues in advance of those of members of her gender and profession. She has a mentality superior to the majority; she has an incorruptible honesty and honor; and she knows how to write."[27]

Although Hellman renounced a successful career in the theater in favor of writing prose, her dramatic skills are evident in the new medium. *Pentimento,* drawing its name from a technique in painting of "seeing and seeing again," was praised for its character portrayals. Hellman presents portraits not of the rich and famous, among whom she moved easily if critically, but of the unknowns who had touched and changed her life, including earthy Bethe, life-loving Uncle Willy, and girlhood friend and anti-Nazi heroine Julia. In lucid, flowing sentences, moving back and forth in time, she attempts to see anew events of the past with the eyes of the present. In trying to understand others, she seeks an understanding of herself.[28]

Scoundrel Time is a dramatic account of Hellman's HUAC hearing, while *Maybe* is somber and fragmented. Treating remembered and half-remembered incidents and persons, the last memoir was praised by some critics, but puzzled those who failed to understand its unconventional style.

Scoundrel Time has been likened to the eye of a storm because Hellman condemns the "cowardice of the self-pro-claimed liberals," the "clowns . . . who just took to the hills" during the McCarthy hearings. Mark W. Estrin believes that the book "reopened among American intellectuals" some "deep political wounds of the past" and that it "triggered what in ret-rospect was almost certainly the beginning of the attack on Hellman's integrity that persists to this day."[29] In 1980, Mary McCarthy, who had long been critical of Hellman's writing and her politics, attacked the veracity of the "Julia" chapter in *Pen-timento.* In 1981 Martha Gellhorn accused Hellman of distor-tion of the facts of the Spanish civil war in *An Unfinished Woman* (1969).[30] In 1986 William Wright wrote a largely neg-ative biography of Hellman because she asked her friends to decline interviews with Wright. Carl Rollyson's *Lillian Hell-man: Her Legend and Her Legacy* (1988) is the most objective biography to date, while *Hellman and Hammett* by Joan Mellen (1996) was judged "grimly negative" by Martha Duffy in *Time* (24 June 1996).

In her later years Hellman suffered from heart trouble and emphysema, no doubt aggravated by constant cigarette smoking that she started in her early teens. Her eyesight failed, and she was declared legally blind. Although she died of heart failure on 30 June 1984, the popularity of her works and interest in her life continues. In the 1996–97 season, there appeared not only a new biography but also on the New York stage a major revival of *The*

Little Foxes, starring Stockard Channing as Regina, and two new plays, *Cakewalk* by Peter Feibleman and *Julia* by Shira Piven. The movie *Dash and Lilly* appeared in 1999.

Artistic Theories and Style

Based upon her own experience with *The Children's Hour,* Lillian Hellman advised students in her writing courses at Harvard and Yale to learn structure by refashioning an existing work. Just as Chekhov's *Three Sisters* had influenced *Toys in the Attic,* she noted, established works could be a springboard for one's own. She taught that each character should have his or her distinctive voice and that subject should determine style. Economy of expression was paramount. A 1961 Harvard student, Ken Stuart, found her a "demanding and inspiring teacher."[31]

The care with which Hellman practiced the precepts she taught is revealed by the drafts, notes, and revisions preserved at the University of Texas Humanities Research Center. Material on *The Little Foxes* includes eight drafts of the play, with lists and descriptions of characters, turns of plot by acts and scenes, and 115 pages of social and historical research for the period.[32] Each draft improves and economizes action and dialogue and sharpens theatrical effect.

Hellman's frequently praised dialogue was due to constant rewriting. "Speech on the stage is not the speech of life, not even the written speech," she reminded an interviewer.[33] *Another Part of the Forest* demonstrates Hellman's instruction to her students that dialogue must reflect and reveal character. Marcus's speech is hard-hitting and forthright; Ben's is trenchant, with sinister undertones; while Oscar's is weak and wandering. Regina's remarks to Marcus are light and musical, fulsome and coquettish, with an insincerity of which Marcus is unaware. Tennessee Williams, seeing *The Little Foxes* on Broadway in 1939, found encouragement for his own plays when he heard Southern dialect used so artistically for the first time on the stage.[34]

Along with the dialogue, Hellman's settings evoke a sense of place and time. *The Little Foxes* set indicates immediately that the Hubbards are rich: "The room is good-looking, the furniture expensive; but it reflects no particular taste. Everything is of the best and that is all." Hellman's modern-day Southern settings in *The Autumn Garden* and *Toys in the Attic* differ from her period locales. In the boardinghouse of *Autumn Garden* can be seen vestiges of its past as a large family home whose air of graciousness is now disturbed by the continuous clatter of implements to sustain the paying guests—brooms, mops, linens, dishes, cups. The oppressive New Orleans heat stifling the sisters at the opening of *Toys in the Attic* permeates not only the hated house but also the action and dialogue.

Hellman's plays are characterized by what Jacob Adler praises as "beautiful clarity of the story line," and "the emergence of the issues, clear and inevitable as sunrise, from the story which illustrates them."[35] Critic Harold Clurman describes Hellman's dramas as "novelistic," and *The Autumn Garden,* which he directed, as having "the density of a big novel," with its interlocking stories of ten people's lives.[36] In her teaching, she assigned Henry James, Anthony Trollope, and Charles Dickens, writers whose strong narrative line, like hers, immediately engages and sustains interest.

In the introduction to *Four Plays* (1942), Hellman notes critics' complaints that her plays are "too well made, the plays are melodramas." She observes that if the violence serves no purpose and points no moral, then the work is open to criticism, but "when violence is the needed stuff of the work and comes toward a large enough end," it is "in the good writer's field." John Gassner states that "since Miss Hellman never employs unmotivated action, she has no need to apologize for her technique." Unlike melodramas, "her own plays . . . invariably employ violence to exemplify and underline the subject, which is the struggle between good and evil in society." She believes in personal responsibility, "contrary to the practice of most writers on social themes."[37]

Hellman admits in the introduction to the initial collection of her first four plays that "there is much in all the plays that is wrong," yet "within the limitations of my own mind and nature, my own understanding, my own knowledge, it was the best I could do with what I had." The "Theatre" chapter in *Pentimento* is her first extended writing on her own plays, and there she focuses on anecdotes rather than analysis.

Few have recognized the humor, irony, and satire in Hellman's works. Her appreciation of Voltaire's satire is apparent in her libretto for *Candide.* In the "Audition Precis," which she prepared for the cast, she praises "the wonderful comedy of the book, the dash, the speed, the roaring-river quality that was the mark of the genius who wrote it. To many it is far the greatest satire ever written, hitting out in all directions, enclosing all human nonsense."[38]

Hellman considered both *The Little Foxes* and *Another Part of the Forest* to be "satiric comedies." Ben and Oscar Hubbard are both outrageous, although Ben can laugh at himself. He is hypocritically playacting about not caring for money in the opening scene of *Foxes.* In *Forest* Oscar declares undying love for a prostitute who scorns him. Mark Estrin observes that as early as *The Little Foxes* Hellman's characters display "clearly sardonic, self-deprecating dialogue."[39] In her 1979 book *Lillian Hellman* Katherine Lederer explores Hellman's use of irony.

Her dramatic technique centers upon contrast and conflict, with the resulting tension rising to a climax. In *Days to Come,* Hellman notes, she gave each leading character a "counterpart." In the later plays, conflict and contrast are intrinsic to the characters from whom the action develops: Regina and Ben, Marcus and Lavinia, Kurt and Teck, Carrie and Anna.

Hellman states in the introduction to *Four Plays* that the theme of both *The Children's Hour* and of *Days to Come* is good and evil. Taking a moral stance toward her subject matter (for which she is often criticized) never diminishes, from the last scene of *The Children's Hour,* when Mrs. Tilford attempts to assuage her guilt with money, to the added "Note" to *Scoundrel Time* in *Three,* again condemning the liberals' failure to take a stand against McCarthy. Robert W. Corrigan notes that Hellman "is interested in showing damnation as a state of the soul, a condition that cannot be reformed out of existence or dissolved by sentimentality or easy optimism."[40]

"A theme common to all her plays [is] that the world we live in is the sum total of the acts of each individual in it. Ignorance, dishonesty and cowardice in personal lives affect social events," observes Katherine Lederer.[41] From the first, Hellman's plays consider the implications of failure to act responsibly. The need for both personal responsibility and self-knowledge are themes of *The Autumn Garden,* one of the best explorations of character in American drama.

John Gassner notes that in *Toys in the Attic,* Hellman "proved again that she could deal with human failure without falling in love with it herself." He adds that "although she looked at life unsentimentally, she combined sympathy with her judgment of the characters." The play reveals that "for people to behave monstrously, it is not even necessary for them to be monstrous, it is sufficient only to be unthinkingly possessive and 'loving.'"[42]

Money is a frequent subject of the plays, with blackmail, theft, and treachery used by characters to gain wealth. Answering critics who claim money is overemphasized in her plays, Hellman responds that she is not alone in treating it as an important issue: it "isn't only money of course, it's power, it's sex; it's a great many other things. It certainly was the subject of Balzac and Stendhal and Dickens and Jane Austen and countless writers."[43] "The presence of money contributes a crackling realism" to Hellman's plays, says Ellen Moers.[44]

"Hellman's sense of place and of people is a strongly Southern one, not simply because much of her childhood was spent in New Orleans but because she intuitively responded to the intense familial and communal relationships she encountered there," observes Richard Poirier.[45] Her plays are family oriented, with the family as the center from which the action emanates.

Deserting drama for memoir gave Hellman the opportunity to expand her technique. To the realistic dialogue and sharp observation that mark her plays she adds in the memoirs poetic rhythms, imagery, free association, and symbolism, along with flowing sentences and dreamlike, surrealistic effects.

Patricia Spacks's observation that Hellman "sees the relation between men and women as a battle" seems too narrow an interpretation, and her statement that Hellman's "central effort has been to create for her own benefit, as well as for others, a character to meet masculine standards,"[46] might well be broadened. Hellman indicates that standards, whether masculine or feminine, should be individual and personal: "You live each day by your own standards, even if you can't require other people to do it. It's as close as you can come to decency, or honesty, or even courage."[47]

Possibly Hellman's most significant contribution to social history and women's studies has gone unnoticed: the faithful chronicle in her plays and memoirs of the position of American women over the eight decades of her life. Some of her themes reflect women's concerns: in the plays, the desire to escape from the restraints of a male-dominated society and the importance of money because of the power it conveys; in the memoirs, dependence and self-doubt.

Much of Hellman's imagery has its basis in the female experience. Some of it is drawn from household and family: "They are mostly people for whom the view from one window, grown dusty with time, has blurred the world," she says of liberals in *Scoundrel Time* (T 723). She writes of her first stay in Hollywood: "I didn't even understand about my marriage, or my life, and had no knowledge of the new twists I was braiding into the kinks I was already bound round with" (UW 60). Asked if she saw many plays: "No. If I'm writing, I have the superstitious belief that you'd better keep the unborn child away from what might harm it."[48]

Hellman compares Chekhov, who disagreed with the staging of his plays, to "a father who is forced to sit in impotent disapproval of his child's adopted home lest if he take the child away a new set of foster parents might prove worse than the old." In a poor production, his characters were like "puff-ball people lying on a dusty table waiting for a wind to roll them off."[49]

Cooking and sewing combine in an image in *Scoundrel Time:* "The CIA was picking up all kinds of clowns on a piece-work basis, and when you work that way the more casseroles you cook up the greater the chance one of them will taste good enough to pay off" (ST 144). Chekhov, she writes, "was unlikely to mistake scorched potatoes for high tragedy."[50] "What fragment at the bottom of the pot was the kettle-spoon scraping that it had not reached before?" she wonders on her return to Russia (UW 166). Dressmaking provides the metaphor of her most famous quotation, about cutting her conscience to fit the current fashion (ST 98).

Bird metaphors, which Ellen Moers observes characterize women's writing, appear in *The Little Foxes* to signify the male characters' domination over Regina. While Regina struggles to free herself, Ben tells her, "Horace has already clipped your wings and very wittily. Do I have to clip them, too?" The character of Birdie in the same play is, as her name implies, fluttery and weak.

As Hellman approached the end of her life, she had written fifty thousand words of a new book and worried the day before she died that it might not be good enough.[51] In the many interviews demanded of her as her fame grew, Hellman constantly regretted that "I wasted too much time." But as the author of thirteen plays, five books of memoirs, eight screenplays, two edited anthologies, and countless articles, "she didn't fritter herself away. She used herself all the time, the best way she could. . . . She was, is, a lasting voice."[52]

CHAPTER TWO

The Children's Hour

"This is not really a play about lesbianism, but about a lie," said Lillian Hellman, describing *The Children's Hour* to a reporter. "The bigger the lie, the better, as always."[1] Opening on Broadway on 20 November 1934, the play centers upon two young women who open a school for girls and are destroyed when a malicious student charges them with lesbianism. By emphasizing the characters of Karen Wright and Martha Dobie and developing action that is as believable as it is theatrical, Hellman drove home her serious theme and achieved, at the age of twenty-nine, an immediate hit that would run for 691 performances.

Because lesbianism was a taboo subject in 1934, the play was banned in Boston, Chicago, and London. Despite its critical and public success in New York and France, it failed to earn the Pulitzer Prize for drama in 1935 because of its subject matter. New York theater critics protested by forming the Drama Critics' Circle, which has been presenting its own awards ever since.

Although *The Children's Hour* was a shocking, controversial play that took courage to write and to produce, it contained certain safeguards that made it morally acceptable. The charge that Karen Wright and Martha Dobie are in a lesbian relationship is untrue, for it is the fabrication of teenager Mary Tilford, a prototypical "bad seed." Karen is in love with and engaged to Dr. Joe Cardin. Martha, who begins to suspect toward the end of the play that she may be a lesbian, commits suicide immediately after sharing that revelation with Karen. In compliance with the 1930s view of homosexuality, she pays with her life for her "crime," an action to satisfy the most conservative audience.

While the sensationalism of the subject had to account in some part for the play's success, Hellman, who considered herself primarily "a moral writer," is concerned here with the harm done by so-called "good people," who do not challenge evil. It is the theme of Hellman's best-known play, *The Little Foxes,* and was to recur in her writing and her life from 1934 on. The character who accepts Mary's lie at face value is her wealthy grandmother, Amelia Tilford, a patron of the school.

Hellman found her plot, at the suggestion of Dashiell Hammett, in a chapter about an Edinburgh lawsuit called "Closed Doors; or, the Great Drumsheugh Case," in *Bad Companions,* a book written by law historian William Roughead. She retained such elements of the original account as the fourteen-year-old student's false charge; her resolute, patrician grandmother; the difficult, interfering aunt of one of the women; and the close relationship between the two teachers—one nervous and high strung and the other stable and placid. Hellman added a fiancé for Karen (to clarify at the onset the fact that the charge is a lie), developed all of the characters, and carried the action forward with ever-increasing tension. The amazing final scene combines the characters' self-revelation and discovery with the kind of theatrical punch that would mark Hellman's plays in the future.

As women are central to Hellman's plays and memoirs, they reflect women's position in society at the time of writing.

Karen and Martha are women who earn their own money and achieve the power and independence this brings. Unlike Regina in *The Little Foxes,* set in 1900, who without money is dependent on what she is given by or can manipulate from men, these women in their late twenties have the teaching and administrative skills that have made the school a success.

Joe, who is more egalitarian than most men were at that time, supports Karen's desire to continue her career after their marriage and respects the women's dedication to the school. In the second scene of act 2, after Mrs. Tilford has summarily withdrawn Mary from the school and warned others to do the same, he champions the women to his aunt: "They've worked eight long years to save enough money to buy that farm, to start that school. They did without everything that young people ought to have . . . That school meant things to them: self-respect, and bread and butter, and honest work."

Young Mary Tilford is so appalling yet mesmerizing a creation that audiences mistook her for the central character and could not understand why she was absent from act 3. Even critics were baffled and faulted Hellman's structuring of the play, but Hellman never intended her as the main character or planned for her to be "the utterly malignant creature which playgoers see in her." Hellman explains that "on the stage a person is twice as villainous as, say, in a novel."[2] The fact that Mary's lie is of a sexual nature intensifies its impact. In the thirties, children, especially girls, were shielded from sexual information and were believed to be uninterested in sex until late puberty. Mary's lie succeeds because adults in her community find it inconceivable that she should know about a lesbian relationship unless she had seen actual evidence of it, and Mary is clever enough to disguise how much she has learned from reading illicit French novels. In telling her story to her grandmother, she gives a convincing portrayal of young innocence unaware of the import of what she is saying. Another reason Mary still has the power to horrify is that Hellman anchors her behavior in reality, drawing upon memories of her own childhood bullying and lying to get her way.[3]

Because Karen is a teacher who believes in being fair and treating the granddaughter of a patron the same as the other students, Mary cannot wheedle her way out when Karen catches her in a lie about picking flowers for Mrs. Mortar, a bouquet she actually found in an ashcan. That Mary will not retreat from so trivial a lie, despite Karen's sympathetic appeals, foreshadows Mary's obduracy in act 2 in defense of her far greater lie. Her blackmailing and bullying of schoolmates in order to run away from the school are also the same techniques she will use in the second act to maintain the lie that allows her the freedom of life with her permissive grandmother.

Mary's grandmother, Amelia Tilford, is a type who will appear regularly in Hellman's plays: the wealthy widow who has been content to be provided for handsomely first by her father and then by her husband. Whether Hellman's portrayal is positive, as it is of Fanny Farrelly in *Watch on the Rhine,* or less sympathetic, as here with Mrs. Tilford, the character is a woman who does not think for herself but has inherited her views, principles, and status from the men in her life. Because her principles are hers only superficially, Mrs. Tilford deserts them when she is confronted with a crisis. One would expect her to investigate Mary's story and to confront Karen and Martha first with what she has heard. However, the lie Mary tells so challenges Mrs. Tilford's concept of the right order of things that after only the most cursory questioning of its truth, she is stampeded into acting. Mrs. Tilford also is led astray by self-righteousness, another failing of which Hellman is critical in the plays. Not only does Amelia Tilford believe her opinions are infallible, but so does the community: when she accepts Mary's lie as truth and alerts the parents, they immediately withdraw their children from the school.

Karen Wright and Martha Dobie command attention and interest almost equally until the end of the play. Although both are competent, intelligent, and committed to their work, they differ in the degree to which they are independent. Martha is less so by virtue of her situation and her temperament. It is Karen's small capital they use to start their venture, a financial disparity that means Martha is not on an equal footing. It is Karen who is more determined to be self-sufficient: she objects when Martha suggests that Karen's fiancé discuss Mary's behavior with his aunt, Mrs. Tilford: "That would be admitting we can't do the job ourselves." On the subject of their retaining Martha's aunt, the incompetent Lily Mortar, Karen can act more firmly. In act 1 she asks Martha outright: "Couldn't we get rid of her soon, Martha? I hate to make it hard on you but she really ought not to be here."

At the close of this conversation, Martha, learning that Karen and Joe plan to marry at the end of the term, is stunned: "You haven't talked of marriage for a long time," as if she had lulled herself into believing that the marriage would never become a reality. Karen's response, "I've talked of it with Joe," again points up the difference between them. Karen has both her close friendship with Martha and an intimate relationship with Joe, another claim on her loyalty and love. Martha has only her friendship with Karen, and is understandably fearful of losing the one relationship that has emotional resonance for her. Their earlier discussion of vacation plans highlights Martha's greater need for Karen and Karen's somewhat unrealistic attitude about the impact her marriage will have on their lives. Martha has envisioned a vacation for just the two of them, like one they had during their college years; Karen's vision is similar, except it is just the three of them. Whether or not Karen is willing to admit it, her marriage *will* make a difference, and Martha's outcry is the anguish of the one who stands to lose the most from the changes it will bring.

To balance Martha's dependency, Hellman endows her with a sharp sense of humor. This is not a play rife with humor; the issues it deals with are too somber for that. But the occasional wit that enlivens the otherwise serious dialogue is usually Martha's. When Joe semijokingly boasts in act 1 that the Tilfords are "a proud old breed," Martha retorts, "The Jukes were an old family, too."

Conversations with Aunt Lily Mortar suggest why Martha is "nervous and highstrung," tense, with low self-esteem. While Amelia Tilford will gain, at enormous cost, understanding and integrity, Mrs. Mortar undergoes no such transformation. Vain and self-centered, a mediocre actress who no longer can find work, she has been hired as an elocution teacher because Martha feels indebted for her upbringing, despite a childhood with Aunt Lily that was neither happy nor comfortable. Seeing herself as a victim in order to put others in the wrong, Lily twists Martha's offer of a pension, if she will leave: "You're turning me out? At my age! Nice grateful girl you are." She does not leave soon enough, for it is her malicious remarks to Martha, overheard by Evelyn and Peggy, that provide the basis for Mary's lie.

Lily Mortar accuses Martha outright of being jealous of Joe and "unnatural" in her affection for Karen, and compounds this by claiming that Martha was "always like that even as a child." Aunt Lily concludes with, "Well, you'd better get a beau of your own now—a woman of your age," an admonition guaranteed to stir anxiety in virtually any woman's heart in those days. Inspired by mere pique, her malice is an assault on Martha's inmost self, and gains unfairly in strength from her role as Martha's surrogate mother, the person, presumably, who has known her best. Her remarks serve to cast Martha's sexuality in an ambiguous light in act 1 and to make Martha's self-revelation and subsequent action in act 3 believable, although nonetheless shocking.

The tragic events Mary's lie sets in motion affect Karen profoundly, but they are external to her. Her essential self remains intact. Philip M. Armato believes Karen lacks compassion for Mrs. Mortar and Mary Tilford and that these characters treat her as she has treated them. He claims Karen's punishment of Mary is unduly harsh and that Mary is justified in feeling persecuted.[4] A careful reading of this scene fails to support this view. Karen is both reasonable and compassionate toward Mary; she also is committed to making a success of her business. Her compassion, therefore, is exercised within the larger context of the school, of ensuring that it is a wholesome environment, with standards of discipline maintained by all students.

Karen's discipline of Mary demonstrates her courage. Given their dependence on Mrs. Tilford's goodwill and financial backing, it would have been easy for Karen to let Mary off with only a token punishment, but she does not. Neither does she shrink from confronting Mrs. Tilford in act 2 to demand an explanation for her abrupt withdrawal of support. Nor in act 3 does she avoid the painful reality that her relationship with Joe is no longer tenable and, with compassion for his anguish, releases him from their engagement.

It is also Karen who has the courage to broach the subject of lesbianism, saying, "But this isn't a new sin they tell us we've done. Other people aren't destroyed by it." But Karen speaks as one for whom the charge is external, imposed on them by the outside world. Martha, on the other hand, internalizes that charge and sees herself through the lens society holds up to her. Underlying the tension characteristic of Martha's personality is a brittleness, at once fragile and rigid, born of her conviction that there is and always has been something radically "wrong" with her. Mary Tilford's lie seems to offer a plausible explanation of the truth about herself.

Despite Martha's wit, her efforts at independence, and her battle against her aunt's attacks, she has achieved neither full self-awareness nor true independence of mind. Hellman explains that "suspecting herself of lesbian desires, not lesbian acts, but lesbian desires, and thus feeling that the charge made against her had some moral truth, although no actual truth," Martha convicts herself of a thought crime and summarily executes herself.[5] The evidence she cites—that she has never felt an intense attachment to anybody but Karen and has "never loved a man"—could be construed as indicating a lesbian cast to her sexuality. Neither the audiences nor critics had any difficulty accepting her judgment at face value. Martha feels she is to blame for the disaster that has befallen them, and yet her claims to that guilt are framed in "I don't know" and "maybe." In one short speech, for example, she repeats the word "maybe" four times, giving the scene a disturbing ambiguity. Judith Olauson observes that the "allegations are believed first by the town, then by friends, and finally by the two women themselves."[6] Martha may be mistaken about herself, for one of the awful powers of such a lie is to convince its victims to believe the image of themselves devised by their oppressors.

Critics saw Hellman as influenced by Ibsen in her careful plotting, social realism, and use of violence. Jacob Adler cites Martha's suicide, Mary's extortion of money from Peggy, and her blackmail of Rosalie as reminiscent of Ibsen's technique.[7] Hellman had a flair for dramatic ways to capture and hold audience attention, but the devices she uses are not for theatricality alone; they are logical extensions of character or situation. In *The Children's Hour,* Mary Lynn Broe observes, "all the truth-revealing scenes are interrupted so that the continuous action of dramatic unraveling and revelation are missing from the play. By such sleight of structure, Hellman shifts the focus from blackmail, extortion, and lesbianism (more melodramatic topics) to the quiet business of redefining a moral capacity."[8] By limiting to the first two acts Mary's presence in the play as the agent of destruction, Hellman in act 3 shifts the audience's attention from the means Mary uses to the wreckage that has resulted from her lie.

With an excellent ear for American speech, Hellman employs language and rhythm to convey character. Her preliminary notes describe Karen as the "voice of reason, straight, clear, dull but educated, balanced, unemotionally awakened."[9] This contrasts with Martha's more fiery, nervous qualities and tension. Their respective dialogue reveals that Karen's speeches are smooth, stable, verging on brisk, and containing no surprises, whereas Martha's are choppy, fragmented, and wry, with unexpected turns. Hellman's use of language to support and underscore action is evident in the final act, for which her notes indicate that "after the suicide, no one must talk with the same words or rhythms as they have before."[10] Through such dislocations of speech, the emotional impact of the tragedy is conveyed, although there is little discussion of the suicide.

The wintry desolation of act 3 is in stark contrast to the hopeful, springtime bustle of act 1, alive with schoolgirls, teachers, and fiancé. A significant drop in energy in act 3 accords with the hopelessness of Karen and Martha, who are the picture of defeat as the act opens, with Karen in an armchair and Martha lying on the sofa. A long two to three minutes of silence indicates to the audience how barren their lives have become. The act proceeds with a further stripping away: first Lily Mortar, then Joe, and finally Martha, so that when Mrs. Tilford arrives to say she has discovered Mary was lying and now wants to make reparations, the irony is complete. Karen's pallid inquiry, "Is it nice out?" hints at the return of hope, and the action comes to a close with commonplaces about the weather signaling the return of normal life.

Not everyone was satisfied with this ending, including Hellman, but she would allow no one else to tinker with her plot. In the course of time, she became convinced that the play should have ended with Martha's suicide. However, for the 1952 revival, she says, "I worked for weeks and weeks trying to take out the last eight or ten minutes of the play, which sounds very easy, as if I could have done it, but I couldn't do it. It had been built into the play . . . so far back, that I finally decided that a mistake was as much a part of you as a non-mistake, and that I had better leave it alone before I ended up with nothing."[11]

The success of *The Children's Hour* opened the door to Hollywood for Hellman as a screenwriter. She adapted the play for the screen as *These Three,* in which she converted the slander to infidelity to satisfy the Hayes Office's strict moral code. In 1962 *The Children's Hour,* with a script by John Michael Hayes from an outline by Hellman, was one of the first movies to be made under the liberalized production codes that replaced the Hayes regulations. In addition to its stagings through the years in the professional and nonprofessional theater, two major revivals were to have an impact. The first was in 1952 during the McCarthy era, with the production and its implications about "the big lie" causing a good deal of controversy, being praised or maligned according to one's political inclinations. In 1995 an acclaimed production by the Royal National

Theatre in London testified to the endurance of "one of the most compelling works to emerge from the serious American theatre before Blanche DuBois and Willy Loman arrived on Broadway in the late 1940s."[12]

CHAPTER THREE

Another Part of the Forest and *The Little Foxes*

"The money-dominated Hubbards" is the subject of *Another Part of the Forest,* which opened 20 November 1946, and *The Little Foxes,* opening 15 February 1939. In this family, writes Hellman, "I had meant the audience to recognize some part of themselves." Acquisitiveness on a personal and on a national scale is the key to the morally reprehensible but theatrically fascinating Hubbard family, distantly related to Hellman's maternal "banking, storekeeping family from Alabama." At their large Sunday dinner gatherings, they talked mostly of profits made from cheating the poor and outwitting the rich (P 180). The vigor and zest with which the Hubbards pursue wealth and the ways they out trick each other to acquire it, Hellman views as comic as well as dangerous. In her teens, she "began to think that greed and the cheating that is its usual companion were comic as well as evil" (P 181). Robert Heilman compares *Foxes* to Ben Jonson's comedy *Volpone,* concerned with "the foxiness of the acquisitive operating against each other."[1] "I had always planned *The Little Foxes* as a trilogy," says Hellman, "knowing that I had jumped into the middle of the life of the Hubbards and would want to go forward in time. But in 1946 it seemed right to go back to their youth, their father and mother, to the period of the Civil War" (P 197). Setting *Another Part of the Forest* in 1880 suggests a parallel between the period after World War II and Reconstruction. *Foxes* takes place in a "small town in the South" and *Forest* is set in Bowden, Alabama. As Hellman looked back through "a giant tangled time-jungle," she could hear "old voices speak about histories made long before my day" (P 172).

Although *Another Part of the Forest* premiered seven years after *The Little Foxes* (1939), here they are analyzed in the chronological order of their settings to reveal the evolution of the characters from youth to middle age. Both plays have been produced in time order on alternate nights, and in 1973 both were published in one volume. Hellman's extensive 115-page research notebook covers the time span of both plays, from 1880–1900. It includes data on architecture, education, songs, fashions, agriculture, industry, politics, and even favorite names.[2] Unifying the two plays is the theme of monetary self-seeking to gain power.

Another Part of the Forest

Before the action of *Another Part of the Forest* begins, Marcus Hubbard was a self-educated mule driver. During the Civil War he prospered, running a store and charging extortionate prices for necessities he acquired by blockade-running. Although Marcus has become well-to-do, son Ben envisions larger gains through ventures emerging in the postwar period. The conflict between Marcus and his strong-willed son grows. A bachelor himself, Ben views marriage by his siblings as one means of building a Hubbard fortune—Oscar's marriage to Birdie would bring with it the Bagtry plantation; Regina must marry Mobile banker

Horace Giddens, a suitor unaware of her scandalous behavior with John Bagtry, who is tiring of the affair.

Reflecting the status of women in that period, Regina, her mother Lavinia, and Birdie have no money and thus no power; they are victims who fall prey to manipulation first by Marcus and then by Ben. Regina, however, attempts to manipulate her father (and in the later play her husband and brothers) to gain power or at least escape from those who dominate her. Oscar is weak, easily outmaneuvered by Ben and his father.

Both parents are complex characters; Marcus, more fully drawn, prizes learning and culture almost as much as he prizes money. He has raised himself from field-worker to landholder, teaching himself Latin and Greek, reading the classics, emulating southern aristocrats with his devotion to music and books and classical arts. With his war profits he purchases the house of a former aristocrat, its style "Southern Greek . . . . a good house built by a man of taste." Yet Marcus is not accepted by the gentry; Colonel Isham will not even drink coffee with him. Both his sons are a disappointment: "one unsuccessful trickster, one proud illiterate." He indulges Regina as long as she flatters him, but he bristles when he learns of her association with John Bagtry. Regina encourages Marcus's favoritism, his endearments suggesting incestuous stirrings. In his sixties, he is aware of his advancing age, and Ben, sensing this softness in his otherwise tough father, plays relentlessly upon the theme of age and death. But Marcus sacrifices sympathy by the way he treats his wife.

In a marriage that was without love from the start, Lavinia shares with her daughter a desire to escape. Yet for the sake of the children, she has remained, not realizing until they are grown that they did not need her. The children have never known love in the family, either from or between their parents. Marcus's cruelty to Lavinia and her references to his "sin" hint of a dark, unshakable curse upon the Hubbards, like that upon the House of Atreus in Greek tragedy. That Marcus is devoted to the Greeks, reads Aristotle, and surrounds himself with classical sculpture is no accident: intending the Hubbard plays to be a trilogy, Hellman had as a contemporary example Eugene O'Neill's *Mourning Becomes Electra,* based upon Aeschylus's *Oresteia.*

Marcus is watchful of Lavinia, for she is (with her black servant Coralee) a witness to his "sin." Returning home from blockade-running, he was followed by Union troops to a secret Confederate training ground where twenty-eight young area men were then massacred. Although Marcus purchased an alibi and even laid the groundwork for declaring Lavinia insane should she reveal the truth, the curse has continued to haunt him in her presence. By the end of the play, the power to hold this knowledge over Marcus has passed to Ben, who, unlike his mother, will be exacting and demanding, having learned well from the example of his father.

The Ben of *The Little Foxes* begins to take shape in *Another Part of the Forest,* where he emerges, full blown, by the end of the play. Earlier, he is wily enough to retain his father's good graces while occasionally riling him, giving hints of the insurrection to come. Ben would have made a superb spy had he not been "bought off" from wartime service. No useful scrap of information is overlooked. Knowing of his father's greed and wishing to ingratiate himself with Birdie, Ben agrees to secure a loan for her; because of his own greed, he doubles the amount, only to have Regina report this to Marcus. To thwart Oscar's intention to marry prostitute Laurette, Ben plies her with liquor during the musicale, knowing that her behavior will evoke Marcus's disapproval.

If, like the rest of the family, Ben had disregarded Lavinia's rambling discourse, he might have lost his chance to acquire Marcus's money and power. But he is alert to her mutterings about Marcus's "sin." His treatment of Marcus in the final act indicates that Ben has studied his father well: the same curt commands, the same alertness to details, the same cold disregard for humanity when money is at stake. Because there is no love in the household, the audience feels no pity for those who end badly, while there is satisfaction that put-upon Lavinia will finally attain her goal: to start a school for black children. Marcus accepts his fate, and Regina and Oscar will continue to be dominated; only the power has changed hands. They will, as Ben wishes them to do, marry for money.

Ben in both plays was inspired by Hellman's great-uncle Jake, a banker brother of her grandmother Sophie Newhouse, whose money he managed. He was a "man of great force, given . . . to breaking the spirit of people for the pleasure of the exercise. But he was also witty and rather worldly, seeing his own financial machinations as natural not only to his but to the country's benefit, and seeing that as comic" (UW 4). Some sympathy is evoked for Ben when he seems to be defeated by Marcus at the end of the second act. Challenged by his father, Ben replies, "I want something for myself. I shouldn't think you were the man to blame me for that." Marcus sneers, "I wouldn't, if you weren't a failure at getting it."

Regina also will have a difficult time explaining to Marcus. Aware of Marcus's emotional dependence, she tells him the truth about Bagtry, threatens to leave forever if her father objects, and then assures the weeping Marcus that nothing will change, despite the planned marriage. She is immature enough to believe she can emotionally control both men.

Twenty-year-old Regina is presented sympathetically; she is inexperienced, willful, giddy, and infatuated with a man who is clearly not in love with her and who is endeavoring to duplicate in Brazil his Civil War glory days. Had Regina not fallen in love with John, no doubt she would have continued as her father's favorite, spending his money lavishly. When Ben's loan to Birdie finances John's trip to Brazil, Regina loses him, but what she wants even more is to escape to Chicago, an escape she still dreams of twenty years later in *Foxes*.

Lavinia too wishes to escape, to start a school in Altaloosa in expiation for not reporting her knowledge of the circumstances leading to the massacre. Like Marcus, she comes from the backwoods. A delicate, nervous woman, she is clearly no match for her husband and children, who treat her as if she were a mentally incompetent child. She is most at home with her servant Coralee, with whom she shares the only caring relationship in the household. Although Lavinia seems submissive and fearful, she has a mind of her own; the self-formed views she holds are in opposition to those of her family and of society. She is both profoundly religious and deeply moral.

Obsessed by the need to atone, Lavinia is sustained by her dream of escaping the Hubbards and returning to her hometown to start her school. Yet her dream depends on Marcus, who continually dismisses her pleas and breaks his promises. Her fear of Marcus can be seen in her eagerness to oblige him and her hesitation in speaking with him, a fear which makes Lavinia nervous and distracted, something of an eccentric. Marcus fosters, for his own protection, the myth that she is crazy. She is, however, not demented. Her descendent is not Blanche in Tennessee Williams's *A Streetcar Named Desire,* as Jacob Adler claims,[3] but rather the fearful and ineffectual housekeeper-cook spinster relative of *The Unsatisfactory Supper* and the films *Cat on a Hot Tin Roof* and *Baby Doll.* (The two latter roles were played by the actress of Lavinia, Mildred Dunnock.) Given the strains placed upon her sanity, Lavinia has done a remarkable job of retaining it.

Although Lavinia admits that she has "spent a life afraid," she recognizes that fear has been imposed upon her: "way down deep I'm a woman who wasn't made to be afraid," she tells Ben at the beginning of act 3. Her courage now begins to surface. Despite Marcus's threats to have her sent to her room or, worse, to have her institutionalized—she grows "daring," he warns—Lavinia persists in taking risks.

In informing the audience that there is in Marcus's past a dark secret or sin, Lavinia acts as a chorus, providing exposition and commentary. When Ben at the end of act 2 craftily mentions "that night," Lavinia expands on the information to include hot tar and clubs and ropes. The suspense as well as the foreboding builds to the beginning of the third act, when Lavinia, goaded by Marcus's disclosure that his promises were "nonsense," reveals to Ben the facts that will give him power over Marcus and his money.

When Ben makes her dream possible, ironically through blackmail in which she unwittingly participates, her departure is touching. No one offers to see her off on her journey or to reciprocate her parting gifts with one for her. She, for whom questions of ethics have genuine meaning, is finally escaping from those with whom she has been forced to live, people whose sole guiding principle is their own self-interest. Birdie is the character most like Lavinia, although there are differences as well. Both are submissive and delicate, but Birdie is not a woman with an independent mind. Although Birdie is a member of the aristocracy and Lavinia is not, they share a helplessness born of powerlessness. As women, they have no money with which to realize their dreams; yet Lavinia, as the stronger character, is able to gain power. Birdie is more helpless; hesitant and fearful, she can, however, muster up the strength to ask the Hubbards for a loan.

Using a favorite technique, Hellman employs contrast in revealing the characters of young Birdie and Regina. Shy and reticent where Regina is forthright and talkative, Birdie is understandably ill at ease with the Hubbards, whom she must ask for money, a situation for which she is unprepared by her former wealth. At the end of act 1 it is not the Bagtrys' desperate plight that inspires Marcus to agree; it is the thought of gaining a prize plantation at such a low price: "Ten thousand is cheap. She's a fool." Ben, who negotiates the loan, sees that by doubling the amount he can acquire money to invest in expanding industries. Though Marcus's main motive is that "it is good for me and bad for them," he appreciates the architecture of the plantation house: "Very light in motive, very well conceived—."

Ben, Marcus, and Regina do not regard Birdie as an individual; they refer to her not by name but as "the girl."

Ben and Oscar contrast with each other, the former too smart and the latter not smart enough. At the end of act 2 Oscar reveals a hellish childhood: "You've bullied me since the day I was born," he tells Ben. Like most cowards, Oscar relies on violence. He rides with the Ku Klux Klan and in act 2 draws a pistol on Ben. Oscar can be cowed easily by Marcus, who docks his meager salary to pay for injuries inflicted by the Klan. Both Oscar and Regina, never having known love in their family, are infatuated rather than in love; the sense of inferiority bred in him by his siblings and father drives Oscar to a prostitute, and his sister finds romance with a weakling, the opposite of her father. In a house full of self-servers, only Lavinia is truly generous, trying, even though she fails, to give and inculcate love to her children.

The structure of a Hellman play is a model of dramatic effectiveness. The action is taut, taking place within forty-eight hours. The dialogue is sharp, as the tension mounts inexorably to a climax in which tricksters are out tricked. Near the end of act 1 Birdie's request for a loan sets the plot in motion, as Lavinia, for the first time, hints of a family sin.

The dialogue in act 1 not only provides the exposition but also establishes character and relationships. Marcus is curt and sarcastic with his sons, whom he obviously despises, indulgent with Regina, and preoccupied or dismissive when addressing Lavinia. Lavinia either interrupts herself or is interrupted by the others. Ben copies his father's manner of speech, especially in put-downs of other family members. But Ben has the saving grace of humor and is able to laugh at himself as well as at others. When thanked by Oscar for providing a fictitious alibi for his Klan scrape, Ben replies: "I wasn't lying for you. I was trying to save five hundred dollars." Regina virtually coos when she addresses her father. She is light and teasing in her chatter with Ben; they vie with each other in insulting Oscar.

Hellman may be recalling the large family dinners of her childhood in the festive family musicale in act 2. This gathering, like the entertainment of Marshall in the first scene of *The Little Foxes,* serves the dramatic purpose of bringing together all of the characters in a showy and stylish atmosphere. In addition, the musicale provides a ritualistic, formal setting within which, by contrast, chaos will erupt at the end of the act. In the background the measured classical music comments ironically on the characters' frantic, self-serving manipulation. Ben plies Laurette with drink; John and Marcus clash; Regina reveals to Marcus Ben's doubling of the loan, and he exposes her plans to elope. Marcus cancels the loan and dismisses Oscar and Ben from the household.

The unfolding plot, in which more and more is revealed about Marcus's sin, comes to a climax and an unexpected resolution in the final act. When Marcus retracts his promises, Lavinia takes her mission into her own hands to expiate the sin she has disclosed to Ben through chance. His clever questioning of her draws out the details of Marcus's role in the massacre, including his payoff for a false alibi. Now Ben may blackmail Marcus into signing over all property to him. He is quick to find Marcus's hoard when Lavinia reveals its whereabouts and to send the loan money to Birdie (including John's fare to Brazil). As Oscar lacks the means to run off with Laurette, and Regina has neither bridegroom nor money to travel to Chicago, they must now accede to the wishes of Ben and "marry money" for him.

The brilliantly theatrical encounter at the end of act 3 between Ben and Regina at breakfast sets the stage for the characters as they appear in *The Little Foxes*. Ben, who holds all the cards, acts with good humor. Regina is demanding and then "bewildered." At first Ben is conciliatory: "It's a shame about you, Regina: beautiful, warm outside, and smart. That should have made a brilliant life. Instead, at twenty, you have to start picking up the pieces, and start mighty fast now." Then Ben becomes cruelly direct: "You can't go away, or at least not on my money, and therefore a willful girl can't have a willful way. You're not in love; I don't think anybody in this family can love."

Ben outlines his plans for his siblings' marriages and for the family fortunes: "Big goings on all over the country. Railroads going across, oil, coal. . . . Things are opening up." Lavinia departs, promising to pray for them all. As the play ends, Marcus asks Regina to pour his coffee. She does so. He indicates the chair next to him. "Regina ignores the movement, crosses to chair near Ben, sits down."

Regina is a survivor; it is the key to her character in both plays. She has more vitality than the other women depicted, yet like them, she is dependent. She will use all her skills to gain what she wants—to marry her lover John and to go to Chicago, away from the Hubbards. She is attractive, clever, self-confident, and manipulative. Neither John nor her father can resist her sexuality, which she will use as the only means she has of attaining power. The play opens in early morning with Regina, clad in nightgown and negligee, coaxing a reluctant John to continue their meetings. But in act 2 at the musicale, when she defies her father, she takes a wrong turn. Then she fails in her pleas with John to elope, and next her ploy against Ben—reporting the real amount of the loan—backfires when Ben reveals her affair with John. Marcus is all but destroyed: "How could you let him touch you?" She must confess to Marcus that she plans to marry John, but promises her father: "John won't worry us. There'll always be you and me—." If she is not just trying to appease Marcus, her tone suggests that she views marriage only as a means of escape. When she threatens to go away and never see him again, Marcus weeps. She has tried to protect her own dreams, but is unable to empathize with John or Marcus.

Another Part of the Forest opened on Broadway 20 November 1946. It was cast and directed by Hellman, with Patricia Neal as a sympathetic, many-faceted Regina. Brooks Atkinson of the *New York Times* called it "demonic," "a witches' brew of blackmail, insanity, cruelty, theft, torture, insult, drunkenness, with a trace of incest thrown in for good measure and some chamber music in the background."[4] In a move judged by some more foolhardy than courageous, Hellman broke the first rule of professional playwrights: never confront a critic. In a letter to the *Times* on 18 December 1946, Hellman replied to Atkinson's review. She implied that his taste was questionable, and stated that her plays had a right to depict violence and evil. To the charge that the play was "contrived," she replied, "I believe that all writing is contrived; some of it is contrived badly."

Among the favorable reviewers was Richard Watts of the *New York Post* (21 November 1946): "A brilliant, distinguished work, of enormous power and impact" was his judgment, noting that Marcus was "not simply a scoundrel but a human being," one whose "striving for culture and scorn for the romantic pretensions of the Confederate South . . . make one understand a great deal about him." Years later Hellman would observe, "If the literary world has a handful of interpreters who mistake themselves for the author, the theatrical world has only a handful who do not mistake themselves for the playwright."[5]

The Little Foxes

A "drama of morality" is Hellman's 1939 description of *The Little Foxes,* which "depict[s] a family just as it was on the way to the achievements which were to bring it wealth or failure, fame or obloquy. At the final curtain the Hubbards are just starting to get on in the world in a big way, but their various futures, individually and collectively, I like to think I leave to the imagination of the audience. I meant to be neither misanthropic nor cynical, merely truthful and realistic." The play is set in the "milling district of the South" because "it was in the cotton states that these years witnessed the sort of exploitation I wanted to write about."[6] In her view of the industrial South at the turn of the century Hellman focuses upon the Hubbards' drive for power through wealth, destroying everything in their path, like the little foxes in *The Song of Solomon* who spoil the vineyards. Hellman is especially accomplished at delivering a moral message in theatrically vivid terms.

Ben Hubbard is an unforgettable individual, epitomizing those who at the turn of the century despoiled the nation for private gain. Schooled by his father to lie, cheat, and steal on a small scale, he is now ready for the big-time opportunities that the industrial age offers, in his case, the bringing of cotton mills to the South. Here huge profits were to be made by exploiting both the natural resources to run the mills and the poor blacks and whites who would work there. Yet Ben is not the "villain" of a melodrama; self-centered, cruel, and heartless, he is also inventive, ironic, and "jolly," a person who can look at events and at himself with a sense of humor. In noting that she had intended that the audience recognize themselves in the "money-dominated Hubbards," Hellman explains in *Pentimento* that she "had not meant people to think of them as villains to whom they had no connection" (P 180).

At his most revealing in the opening scene, Ben is now fifty-five, "with a large jovial face and the light graceful movements that one often finds in large men." He states the case for the Hubbards, who were in trade when the Civil War broke out. While the southern aristocrat failed to change with the times, the Hubbards did so: *"Our* grandfather and *our* father learned the new ways and learned how to make them pay." Then Ben hypocritically adds to the family history, "A man ain't only in business for what he can get out of it. It's got to give him something here. (*Puts hand to his breast.*) . . . Money isn't all." Their new partner from the North, Marshall, who may act more gentlemanly than Ben but is just as greedy, replies, "Really? Well, I always thought it was a great deal." Hellman's notes for Ben as she drafted the play describe him as "big, calmer, and more talkative than the rest. He and Regina are smarter than the others and always have been."[7]

Regina, the central character of this play, is now a handsome woman of forty, retaining the vitality, good looks, and intelligence of the young Regina of *Forest,* but now more shrewd, self-controlled, and dangerous. In the first scene she demonstrates the graces of southern womanhood. She flatters Marshall, steers the conversation away from perilous topics, smooths over awkward patches, and exerts her charm and sexual magnetism to assure Marshall that he is not only welcome but personally attractive to her. She sees him as one who will open doors, who has promised to show her around Chicago, and whose wife will be the very person to introduce her to the right people.

In the well-orchestrated sequence that follows, the family speaks aloud the private dreams that wealth will enable them to realize. Both Birdie and Oscar are shocked by Regina's intention to leave for Chicago and then Paris. In her planning-stage notes for Regina, Hellman says: "Perhaps all through play wants to move to bigger town."[8] In *Pentimento* she describes Regina as "a woman who had all her life been on her way to another house" (254). Oscar is shocked and Birdie dismayed, fearing that Regina's husband, Horace, will be too ill to travel. As her vision does not include Horace, Regina simply ignores Birdie's objection. Ben takes Regina's dream in stride, remarking, "She is going to see the great world and leave us in the little one. Well, we'll come and visit you and meet all the great and be proud you are our sister." Initially, Ben's good nature seems inspired by Regina's understanding and admiration for his accomplishments, but it is soon apparent that he is toying with her. He lets her soar on the wings of her dream and then pulls her sharply to earth with the threat that she will have no share in the millions unless Horace agrees to invest with them.

Although Regina has no money and consequently no power, she does have a quick intelligence and an understanding of both Ben and Oscar. She is able to transform Ben's insinuation that Horace isn't interested in their scheme from a threat into a ploy to gain a larger percentage for Horace and herself. Having listened well and often to her brothers and learned from their techniques, she is too clever to presume equality, not even with Oscar. As act 1 draws to a close, she plays the role of the helpless woman who knows nothing about business: "I don't know about these things," she begins, throwing them off guard, flattering them that they know so much more. "I should think that if you knew your money was very badly needed, well, you just might say, I want more, I want a bigger share. You boys have done that." Ben admires Regina's maneuvers, especially since he now knows that she will convince Horace to invest with them.

It is important to Ben that Regina remain in the mold of the helpless woman, as he keeps reminding her. To seize the advantage, he remarks at the end of act 1, is "not pretty, Regina, not pretty." Or he may caution her, in act 2, not to frown as she follows Horace up the stairs to continue their argument: "Softness and a smile do more to the heart of men." The tone of the argument offstage indicates that Regina has ignored Ben's advice. On the threshold of realizing her most cherished dreams, she abandons the role of helplessness and speaks in her own insistent, demanding voice—and fails.

She fails to persuade Ben to wait any longer, and when, at the end of act 2, she demands that he do so, Ben warns her, "Since when do I take orders from you?" Next she fails with Horace, who knows he is dying but resolves to do no more harm: "I'll die my own way. And I'll do it without making the world any worse. I leave that to you." Defeated and desperate, despairing of her dream, Regina responds by voicing and not concealing what she sees as her only way out: "I hope you die soon."

There is worse to come for Regina in act 3. Even her hope of inheriting money when Horace dies is dashed when Horace discovers that Leo has stolen the bonds and informs Regina that he is making a new will, leaving her only the bonds on loan to her brothers. The bulk of his estate will go to their daughter, Alexandra.

Regina sees this as vindictive and vengeful on Horace's part: "You are punishing me." Horace reminds her that she is powerless: "You won't do anything. Because you can't." As the bonds are a loan, he says, "for once in your life I am tying your hands." (The cruel metaphor reminds Regina that, like all women of her day, her disadvantage is both financial and physical.) "Ben will think it all a capital joke on you," says her husband, and reminds her that she has no power: "There's nothing you can do to them, nothing you can do to me." After Horace's "punishing" revenge, Regina has nothing more to lose.

Hellman carefully motivates Regina's passiveness while Horace suffers a heart attack, having broken one bottle of crucial medicine and calling for the other, which is upstairs. The seizure is precipitated by Regina's striking back after Horace's revenge. Remembering Horace's earlier flings with "fancy women,"[9] she attacks his sexual vanity: she has never loved him; he always has been sexually unattractive to her. She despised Horace for believing the doctor advised her that her husband should not touch her anymore. If Horace is not to change his will and deprive her of her last opportunity to lead an independent life, there is little time left.

Because she is desperate, because her last hope of escape has been dashed with a small inheritance that she will not even own until Ben is ready to return the bonds, because Horace has cruelly enjoyed tying her hands so that she can do nothing except watch her brothers grow richer, because she knows how much is at stake, Regina can stand by silently while Horace suffers a fatal heart attack. The most recent actress of Regina on Broadway, Stockard Channing, convincingly, and more humanly, interpreted this moment for Regina as an emotional near-breaking point, while for predecessors Tallulah Bankhead and Bette Davis it was an instance of triumph. Bankhead, the original Regina, so stamped her view of the role as a cross between Clytemnestra and Lady Macbeth that all of the reviewers shared her interpretation. Davis gave a similar one-dimensional performance in the movie version, where Herbert Marshall depicted Horace as a saint.

As the play draws to its close, it remains only for Regina to turn the tables on Ben and Oscar. Her husband having died before he could change his will, she not only inherits his money but also blackmails Ben and Oscar into 75 percent of the Hubbard share of the mill. If they do not agree, she need only disclose the theft to send them to jail. She is no longer the helpless woman, claiming no knowledge of business. She has the power the inheritance bestows upon her, and warns them, "As long as you boys both behave yourselves, I've forgotten that we ever even talked about them [the bonds]. You can draw up the necessary papers tomorrow." She reminds Ben, as he once did their father, that he is getting old and that his tricks are losing their bite.

As Ben and Regina laugh, she compliments him on being a good loser. Ben says he isn't discouraged: "The century's turning, the world is open. Open for people like you and me. Ready for us, waiting for us." Even though their names may be different, they are Hubbards and will own the country one day. And he slyly reminds Regina of the possibility of future blackmail: "What is a man in a wheelchair doing on a staircase?" Regina's enigmatic comment suggests that things might have been different: "Ah, Ben, if Papa had only left me his money."

The situation of a wife refusing to aid an ill, dying husband appears in two precedents familiar to Hellman. In Henry James's *The American,* an influence, Hellman notes, on *Watch on the Rhine* (P 185), the American hero is thwarted in his courtship of a noble Frenchwoman because of a dark family secret. He loses his fiancée but he discovers the secret: her mother caused her ill husband's death by depriving him of the only medicine that would prevent it. In Eugene O'Neill's 1929 Broadway play *Mourning Becomes Electra,* based upon the *Oresteia,* the wife Christine (Clytemnestra) actually substitutes poison when her ill husband Mannon (Agamemnon) calls for his medicine and then she watches him die.

Hellman again uses contrast to sharpen the characterization of Regina and Birdie, now middle aged. In the opening scene of *Foxes* Ben brags to Marshall of acquiring from the aristocracy "their land, their cotton, and their daughter." He speaks of Birdie as property, and third on the list at that, one of the spoils of success. That humiliation is a staple of Birdie's life is apparent all through the opening act, which ends with Oscar's striking her.

Birdie's only defense against the trials of the present is her preoccupation with her happy past. At the beginning of act 3, with Alexandra, Addie, and Horace, Birdie recalls bygone days: "If we could only go back to Lionnet. Everybody'd be better there." When Alexandra (affectionately called Zan) asks why she married Oscar, Birdie says: "Ben Hubbard wanted the cotton and Oscar Hubbard married it for him. . . . Everybody knew that's what he married me for. Everybody but me. Stupid, stupid me."

Another escape for Birdie is in drink, she confesses, yet she warns Zan that she could be the same in twenty years. When Addie remarks upon Birdie's outspokenness, Horace's reply indicates that the course of the play is, in effect, a rite of passage for Zan: "Let her listen now. Let her see everything. How else is she going to know that she's got to get away?"

In the opening scene Alexandra is like a child at her first grown-up party, described as pretty and rather delicate, a well-behaved girl of seventeen. Hellman notes that "I had meant to half-mock my own youthful high-class innocence in Alexandra" (P 180). Zan, being sent alone to fetch her father, gives the first evidence that she is capable of disobeying Regina: if he is too ill to travel, she says, she will not have him do so. Returning in act 2, Alexandra reveals that the trip and its responsibilities have matured her. She is the fledgling adult, fussing around her father and giving instructions to Addie, delighted to be of service, to be competent and responsible, and yet not fully in charge of her life. She is horrified at the bitter exchange between her parents, and from her efforts to shield her father, it is clear where Zan's allegiance lies.

The course of act 3 completes Alexandra's transition from child to young adult. As Birdie has warned Zan of the personal dangers, so Addie apprises her of the larger dangers if she remains with the Hubbards: "Well, there are people who eat the earth and eat all the people on it like in the Bible with the locusts. And other people who stand around and watch them eat it. *(Softly)* Sometimes I think it ain't right to stand and watch them do it."

Alexandra will remember these words as she makes the final break with Regina at the end of the play. Zan has witnessed her mother's coup over her brothers and the cold conversation among these relatives who have lived in each other's pockets all their lives. Trying to be as kind to her daughter as she was tough with her brothers, Regina remembers her own, thwarted youth: "You shall have all the things I wanted. I'll make the world for you the way I wanted it to be for me." But Alexandra realizes the price is too high: "I am going away from you. Because I want to. Because I know Papa would want me to." Her daughter, Regina decides, will not be deprived of the freedom and independence she has sought all her life and which only now, with money and power, have become possible: "Somewhere there has to be what I want, too. Life goes too fast. Do what you want; think what you want; go where you want." Regina sums up her girlhood: "Too many people used to make me do too many things."

As the impetus for her future direction, Alexandra recalls Addie's words about those who eat the earth. She asks Regina to tell Ben that "I'm not going to stand around and watch you do it. I'll be fighting as hard as he'll be fighting . . . someplace else." Regina's response shows her admiration: "Well, you have spirit, after all. I used to think you were all sugar water."[10] Having gained the power to control her brothers, Regina has lost control over her daughter, for this will not depend upon money. The best she can hope for in her isolation is to be friends: "I don't want us to be bad friends, Alexandra." The play ends, as does *Forest,* with an invitation rejected; for the first time, Regina is hesitant: "Would you—would you like to sleep in my room tonight?" Alexandra's response, unlike the young Regina's expediency, is chilling: "Are you afraid, Mama?" as her mother climbs the stairs alone.

If Birdie is too weak and Regina too strong, Alexandra represents a whole woman, combining Birdie's warmth and caring with Regina's determination and spirit. Grandmother Lavinia, mother Regina, and daughter Alexandra all share a desire to escape from life with the Hubbards, and each attains her escape, at a price. According to Hellman's plan for a trilogy, Alexandra was to be the central character of the third play (which she did not write) set in Europe in 1925: "Maybe a spinsterish social worker, disappointed, a rather angry woman."[11]

Hellman believed and taught that dialogue should reflect the character of the speaker. One would expect Ben's speech to be curt and masterful, as he is; Oscar, slower witted, is more hesitant in his dialogue. Both, basically uneducated, fall back on clichés. Yet Ben, like Volpone, waxes rhapsodic when he speaks of wealth to Horace in act 2: "I've always said that every one of us little Southern businessmen had great things . . . right beyond our fingertips. It's been my dream: my dream to make those fingers grow longer."

In act 3, when Regina states that Horace intends the bonds to be a loan, Ben responds: "Horace has already clipped your wings and very wittily. Do I have to clip them, too?" Although a cliché, Ben's metaphor is apt, for it suggests that Regina has been like a caged bird and now will be denied all possibility of flight.

Birdie's dialogue with Oscar is querulous and repetitious: "What am I doing? I am not doing anything. What am I doing?" But in act 1, when each expresses a wish for the wealthy future ahead, she speaks lyrically of restoring Lionnet to its former glory. Although Horace says little, he is given an aria at the end of act 2 to repent his earlier Hubbard dealings: "Why should I give you the money? (*Very angrily*) To pound the bones of this town to make dividends for you to spend?" Charlotte Goodman observes that the speech patterns of *The Little Foxes* may well have encouraged Tennessee Williams's lyrical southern speech in *The Glass Menagerie*.[12] Lyle Leverich reports that in 1939 Williams saw *The Little Foxes* in New York and that it "impressed Tom deeply."[13]

Despite the play's good reviews, Hellman laments the dearth of helpful criticism: "I wanted, I needed an interesting critical mind to tell what I had done beyond the limited amount I could see for myself. But the high praise and the reservations seemed to me stale stuff and I think were one of the reasons the great success of the play sent me into a wasteful, ridiculous depression. . . . trying to figure out what I had wanted to say and why some of it got lost" (P 179–80).

CHAPTER FOUR

Watch on the Rhine

Watch on the Rhine, which opened 1 April 1941, was a call to arms to the American public, who, Hellman felt, were too complacent about the menace of Fascism, which she had experienced firsthand in the Spanish civil war. Like Bertolt Brecht, Mark Estrin notes, Hellman "expects her audience to be enraged enough by the injustice she dramatizes to leave the theatre and take social action."[1] As might be expected, the play did not generate an immediate reversal of American political policy, but it did have an impact on American thinking as an influential work rallying support for the allies. In October 1941 the Free World Association broadcast the play in German via shortwave to Germany in a special performance from backstage, with Mady Christians repeating her role as Sara and Otto Preminger as Kurt.[2]

Eight months after *Watch on the Rhine* opened, the Japanese bombed Pearl Harbor, precipitating America's entry into World War II. From its opening night to its closing 378 performances later in February 1942, audiences responded enthusiastically. Critic Stark Young was more reserved: "some of the first act appears to lose time or wander too amiably—for one instance, perhaps with the scene of the children in which so many lines are given to Bodo, the comical, pedantic little boy" (*The New Republic,* 14 April 1941). Wolcott Gibbs of *The New Yorker* judged it "a fine honest and necessary play in which the fundamental issue of our time has been treated with dignity, insight, and sound theatrical intelligence."[3] The play earned the New York Drama Critics' "best play" award and in January appeared in a command performance at the White House, for "the first public appearance of President Roosevelt since war had been declared" (P 194). London and Moscow performances followed, and in 1942 and 1943, after the Broadway production closed, *Watch on the Rhine* was staged in regional theaters across America.

Feeling that "her writing had to spring from a completely realized world, the kind a novelist presents," Hellman researched the play carefully, amassing material on every aspect of German life. Margaret Case Harriman was so impressed with Hellman's careful, voluminous notes that she believed they "could be expanded . . . into a detailed and accurate history of a period covering 25 years."[4] The actual writing of the play went smoothly, says Hellman: "The only play I have ever written that came out in one piece, as if I had seen a landscape and never altered the trees or the seasons of their colors" (P 193).

For her approach, Hellman used Henry James's contrast in *The American* and *The Europeans* between worldly wise Europeans and naive, well-meaning Americans. The play is family oriented, centering upon the Americans, the Farrellys, and set in their spacious, well-appointed home in the suburbs of Washington, D.C. Matriarch Fanny presides over the household; her son David, an attorney, lives with her. The action begins when her daughter Sara, who has left home to marry German anti-Fascist Kurt Muller, arrives from Europe with him and their three children. Another American is Marthe, forced into a loveless marriage to a Rumanian count by her mother, dazzled by his title. The Farrellys have not inquired into the background of the count, who, with Marthe, has been their houseguest for six weeks. Count Teck de Brancovis and Kurt are immediately suspicious of each other. A friend of the Nazi officials at the German embassy in Washington, Teck is down on his luck and nearly penniless. He suspects there is a price on Kurt's head as an anti-Fascist leader, whom he could betray to the Nazis, and further learns that Kurt is carrying $23,000, "gathered from the pennies of the poor," to finance the resistance. Their conflict forms the basis of the action, with a romantic subplot involving David Farrelly and Marthe. As the tension increases, it becomes clear it is a conflict that can be resolved only by the death of one of the men.

Teck de Brancovis is a man of no substance, neither material nor moral. His quest for money and power has long since eroded any scruples he ever had, and he is perfectly willing to play cards with Nazis and Americans who sell illegal armaments. Hellman based his character on Rumanian Prince Antoine Bibesco, a practiced cardsharp who fleeced her of some six hundred dollars at the London home of Lady Margot Asquith in 1936 (P 187–90). Teck too is a cardsharp who relies on the game as a major source of income and looks to be useful to his unsavory associates in the hopes of regaining access to power.

The Muller family no sooner arrives in act 1 than Teck senses there is profit to be made from learning as much as possible about Kurt, Fanny's unlikely son-in-law, "a German who has bullet scars on his face and broken bones in his hands" and whose luggage is unlocked, while a shabby briefcase is carefully locked. Sure that he is on the scent of someone the Nazis would pay to know about, Teck investigates the Muller baggage at the first opportunity. News of the capture of other important resistance leaders jogs Teck's memory. He realizes that Kurt is now at the top of the Nazis' most wanted list and attempts to blackmail him, offering him, in return for ten thousand dollars, a month of silence in which to try to return to Germany to rescue his comrades. Kurt, however, knows, as Fanny and David do not, of Teck's unsavory background in Europe and that his offer of silence is purest sham. He is a deadly threat to Kurt and Kurt's colleagues, and before he can betray them to their deaths, he must be killed. Through Teck, the audience sees that the charm, the culture, the polish of some European aristocracy masks a rotten core. Whatever last tatters of decency Teck displays in his farewell to Marthe and his excuses to the Farrellys, he remains a man who will sell anyone and anything for personal advantage, a dangerous enemy who must be eliminated.

Unlike Marthe and Teck, Sara and Kurt are an American/ European combination that embodies that which is best in both worlds. They respect each other, their love is as fresh as when they first met twenty years ago, and their children are warm and courteous. The heroic figure of Kurt Muller is based, Hellman says, on her beloved friend Julia, who devoted her wealth, her intelligence, and even her life to fight Fascism (P 187). The choice to make Kurt a German indicates Hellman's acknowledgment that not all Germans slavishly followed Hitler. She further avoids a simplistic view of Germany and even of Fascists through Kurt's continuing pride in his country "for that which is good" and the hope he expresses of bringing the Farrellys to Europe after the war to "show them what Germany can be like." In response to Teck's observation in act 3 that "there is a deep sickness in the German character . . . a pain-love, a death-love," Kurt offers an analysis that recognizes gradations among Fascists: "There are those who give the orders, those who carry out the orders, those who watch the orders being carried out . . . Frequently they come in high places and wish now only to survive. They came late: some because they did not jump in time, some because they were stupid, some because they were shocked at the crudity of the German evil, and preferred their own evils, and some because they were fastidious men." For the last group, he says, "we may well someday have pity."

In speaking of Hellman's "mature realism," Timothy Wiles points out that she "avoids a doctrinaire explanation for the Nazi's evil ascendancy based simply on economics, and dramatizes social forces like the authoritarian personality and ideas like the banality of evil." She recognizes Fascism as "a psychological force that could be unleashed in the mass mind by its proponents' conscious manipulation of racial hatred."[5] At no point does Hellman underestimate the evil the Nazis represent, and Kurt's speech is not intended to mitigate that evil. In fact, when Teck tells Kurt, "You have an understanding heart," Kurt rejoins, "I will watch it." Hellman's intention is to show that an evil of such magnitude comprises a broad spectrum of human frailties, which makes it even more dangerous.

On a personal level, Kurt Muller is a charming, mature, acutely intelligent man who can hold his own with a forceful personality like Fanny Farrelly. His love for his family is profound, and he is very much aware that his work to guarantee their future has entailed the sacrifice of his children's childhood. By this revelation in act 3, the audience is aware that no such option as a normal childhood exists under the circumstances, and the life they have had is at least one of honor, decency, and hope.

One of Kurt's most appealing qualities is his love for his wife: he encourages her to enjoy the pleasures of her family home without fear of offending him; he respects and praises all her contributions to their partnership, and his love for her is both tender and yet still charged with sexual ardor. In act 2, when he knows he must return to Germany because of the capture of his colleagues, he draws Sara to him, saying, "How many years have I loved that face?" and then "kisses her, as if it were important," unheeding of the others in the room. It is a powerful display of lasting romantic love.

The major hallmarks of Kurt's heroism are his honesty and personal integrity. Hellman deliberately avoids affiliating him with any particular party, thereby removing the audience's option to disassociate from him on the basis of political prejudices, and it seems fair to assume that this was also the reason she includes no reference to anti-Semitism. Instead, Kurt is an Everyman, representing the potential in each person to respond to the call of conscience. He speaks movingly of the Spanish civil war, where he fought as a member of the German brigade. For Kurt, August 1931, when he saw "twenty-seven men murdered in a Nazi street fight" in his hometown, marked the end of passive hope and the beginning of action. He concludes the story, saying, "I remember Luther, 'Here I stand. I can do nothing else. God help me. Amen.'"

Repeatedly, Kurt brings the issue down to personal responsibility, a recurrent theme in Hellman's plays. When Fanny and David try to dissuade him from returning to almost certain death by citing his family as a reason to stay, Kurt points out that each man has a reason not to fight, yet each must sleep with his conscience. The fact that he is a vulnerable man whose hands, broken by torture, shake when he is afraid, and who admits to the fear he feels, only underscores his heroism. Kurt's courage and determination send the message, as David says in act 2, that "it's the way all of us should feel." And Kurt, who hates violence, makes sure there is no glossing over his murder of Teck, that his children know this is not the way their world should be. His leave-taking ends on an optimistic yet uncertain note, for the prospects for survival are dismal for so likable and courageous a man.

Sara Muller is the ideal wife and mother of the forties. In direct contrast to Marthe, Sara is the American girl of independent spirit who defied her mother and chose her husband for love, not status and wealth. Her mother is shocked to learn that Sara worked to support her family, enabling Kurt to pursue his anti-Fascist work, and says the Farrellys would gladly have sent money had it been requested. Yet Sara's convictions are Kurt's; her passionate espousal of his ideals is indistinguishable from her profound love for him. There is a satellite quality to both Sara's opinions and her status in her family. She explains to Fanny and David, "I wanted it the way Kurt wanted it," a combination of political and moral ideals and deep love for her husband. She may indeed be as Kurt describes her, "brave and good . . . handsome and gay"; nonetheless, she is still only a "good girl," as her brother so approvingly remarks when she says she wants Kurt to go, to save the people so important to him and to their cause.

Although their parts are minor, the children make important contributions to the play. They represent the most powerful motive of all for mounting the fight against Fascism, the future of the world's children. They serve less lofty purposes as well. In their innocence they remark on the wonders of American life, simultaneously flattering an American audience on their standard of living and revealing the harsh circumstances under which the Mullers have been existing. Babette's shy request for an egg for breakfast, "if an egg is not too rare or too expensive," makes their deprivations vividly real. The eldest, Joshua, invites Fanny to practice her languages with them as they "speak ignorantly, but much, in German, Italian, Spanish—." These pieces of information from the children picture the life the Mullers have been forced to live under Hitler and relieve Kurt of having to do so.

Individually, they are stereotypically fine young people. Joshua intends to carry on his father's fight against Fascism. Babette, like her mother, puts a brave face on hardships. Bodo, the youngest, is a funny little boy, self-confident, enchanted with grand words, and thoroughly convinced that his father is the greatest hero on earth. His age makes it appropriate for him to inadvertently reveal important information, and also allows him to sing his father's praises freely. His main function, however, is to transmit Kurt's philosophical and political beliefs in such a way as to make them accessible without the sententiousness they might have were an older person to deliver them. He makes pompous little speeches that are obvious echoes of his father's views, but Bodo's stilted English, filled with big words, often mispronounced, gives them a lighter, slightly comical flavor. Hellman thus gets across important ideological messages without diminishing their significance or boring the audience. If anything, Kurt's beliefs are enhanced by Bodo's endearing delivery of them.

Described as "a handsome woman of about sixty-three," Fanny Farrelly is a woman of strong, vivid personality who has enjoyed wealth and status all her life. Her father had been an ambassador and her husband, the late "famous Joshua Farrelly," was ambassador to France in addition to founding a distinguished law firm. Her life has been as rich in experience as in material comforts, and the deep love she and her husband had for one another is a source of happy memories and a point of pride with her. He remains the yardstick by which all men, especially her son David, are to be measured.

Since traditional ideals of romantic love, marriage, and family, and women's place in relation to them underpin the structure of this play, it is appropriate that Fanny Farrelly adored her husband while he was alive and cherishes his memory after his death. She represents a certain idea of the feminine that audiences at that time found particularly sympathetic, that of a woman who, while very much a distinctive personality in her own right, is yet quite happy to defer to her husband and to play a subordinate role. As Vivian Patraka points out, the appeal of romantic love surviving intact would divert most women today from the realities such a relationship implies.[6] Fanny's frequent references to Joshua Farrelly make him an almost palpable presence in the play. Although Fanny may be a widow, she is not alone; the husband who was the source of her status still validates that status and attenuates her authority as matriarch. Fanny is free to speak as she pleases because she does not violate traditional ideas of womanly behavior and woman's place within the family.

Much of the humor of the play derives from Fanny's outspokenness and her capricious behavior. She expresses her opinions freely, even bluntly, as when she surveys her grandchildren for the first time. She compliments Joshua on bearing the name and looks of his grandfather, praises Babette, and then to nine-year-old Bodo remarks, "You look like nobody." Fanny and her son David embody characteristics generally recognized as American, and most of these are flattering to the national image. Fanny's candor and individuality, her self-confidence, and her generosity are such. However, Hellman's intention in *Watch on the Rhine* is not simply to mirror that which is admirable in the American character but to move Americans from a stance she considers dangerously naive.

This naïveté is displayed by both Fanny and David. Fanny has invited the count and Marthe as houseguests because, she explains to David in act 1, "I felt sorry for Marthe, and Teck rather amused me. He plays good cribbage and tells good jokes." Despite her years as an ambassador's wife, Fanny remains naive in her judgment of Europeans, and her superficial assessment of Teck proves a dangerous mistake. When she rebukes Kurt for carelessness in leaving thousands lying around, he points out that the money was in a locked briefcase, concluding, "It was careless of you to have in your house a man who opens baggage and blackmails." Her carelessness is of a piece with her role in life. Political convictions were her husband's province. Her job was to be charming, to garner gossip, "wit it up," and pass it along entertainingly. Fanny's antics do double, even triple, service. They are comic relief to the play's more serious theme, they mitigate Fanny's status as an authority figure so that she remains sympathetic, and they indicate an area where change and growth are needed. For Fanny will be capable of mature behavior when the need arises. As act 3 draws to a close, she rallies behind Kurt and his cause, signaling her support of him with that highest of accolades, a quotation from husband Joshua. She also stands prepared to take responsibility for helping Kurt hide the murdered Teck and to escape the country.

Her son David has not been able to assert himself because of his flawed self-esteem. The source of his difficulty may lie in Fanny's habitually comparing him to his father and his choosing to believe her judgments of him. His love for and defense of Marthe strengthens his resolve, as he does not permit Teck to bully her nor does he allow Fanny to interfere, as she has in the past, with his relationships. By the play's end he understands the dangers Kurt faces and is prepared to aid him. David has become a strong, mature, independent adult. When Fanny says to David at the end of act 3, "Well, here we are. We are shaken out of the magnolias, eh?" it is clear that they are now aware of the dangerous realities that lurk just beneath the surface of life as they have previously known it. When David warns her that trouble lies ahead, she replies that she understands: "We will manage. I'm not put together with flour paste. And neither are you—I am happy to learn."

Structurally, *Watch on the Rhine* is an interweaving of contrasts; the lighter comedic threads of Fanny's outbursts and sharp humor and Bodo's grandiose speeches provide relief from, and at the same time intensify the effect of, the darker strands of menace. The opening act is predominantly light, with the warmth of the reunion, yet darker notes sound with the threat posed by Teck's curiosity. Act 2, set ten days later, when relationships have developed, opens in a light, comic vein but darkens midway with the news of the capture of Kurt's comrades and Teck's attempt at blackmail. The final act reverses the first and is a crescendo of darkness relieved briefly by one or two comic touches and by the warmth of Kurt's love for his family, and finally by the resolve of all to fight Fascism, despite the cost.

In 1942 the movie of *Watch on the Rhine* was scripted by Dashiell Hammett, with additional scenes by Hellman. Paul Lucas repeated his Broadway role of Kurt, and Bette Davis played Sara. One last hurdle Hellman had to overcome was the Breen Office stipulation that murder be punished, that Kurt be assassinated in retaliation for his killing Teck. Her letter to the censors, whom she complained to the producer were "not only as unintelligent as they were in the old days, but . . . growing downright immoral," was characteristically caustic: the country was at war with the Nazis. Should American soldiers who killed Nazis also pay with their lives?[7] The film still stands as a classic example of American cinematography. Although its revival in 1979 was considered "dated" by the critics, the play represents one of the best of the pro-war dramas, one which translated the panorama of "historical events and emotions connected to them" into the smaller, more accessible frame of the family, so that the spectator can "internalize and internationalize what [is] now recreated as a domestic crisis."[8] Much as *The Diary of Anne Frank* made the fate of millions a palpable reality through a single girl, *Watch on the Rhine* , through its focus on a family in early 1941, made Americans aware of the threat to their security.

CHAPTER FIVE

The Autumn Garden

The Autumn Garden, which opened on Broadway 7 March 1951, was a radical departure in style and focus from Hellman's earlier tightly plotted plays that concentrated on conflicts between characters and on urgent moral or social issues. Critics saw the play as a shift from the social realism of Ibsen to the character exploration of Chekhov; although, as Mark Estrin points out, "the reflective, rueful voice [of *The Autumn Garden*] had its structural roots not in Chekhov, but in the discursive elements within *Watch on the Rhine, The Searching Wind,* and *Another Part of the Forest.*"[1] Few plays before or after *The Autumn Garden* have explored character so deeply, presenting individuals so convincingly that one is reminded of friends or relatives or even of oneself. At the same time, these seven people in the autumn of their lives are universal in their awareness of the passage of time and of their need to reassess their past and their choices made and to be made.

In an interview with Vernon Rice of *The New York Post,* Hellman explained the title: "An autumn garden is one which by winter time will fade and not be a garden any more. It's a chrysanthemum garden. The people in the play are coming into the winter of life" (6 March 1951). The play's structure is consonant with autumn's muted colors and diffuse light. Instead of focusing sharply on a central character or issue, Hellman softens and widens the focus among several characters, interweaving their stories to create a novelistic effect of richness and depth. Action such as there is partakes more of the nature of incident than of event. There are no prolonged dramatic confrontations or resolutions of conflict, but the play is far from static. Hellman "supplies the external tension, a tension partly produced by confusion and stir, but a tension which accurately mirrors the inner states of mind and emotions of the characters."[2]

Six of the major characters are on stage at the opening of the play. They are in the living room of the Tuckerman guest house, once a spacious private home "in a small summer resort town on the Gulf of Mexico about a hundred miles from New Orleans in September 1949." When the curtain rises, they are gathered after dinner. Their conversation indicates they are comfortable with each other and have spent many such evenings together. All of them have been summering at Constance Tuckerman's resort for many years. Carrie Ellis, who comes every year with her son Frederick and her elderly mother-in-law, Mary, has known Constance since high school. So has Ned Crossman, who has long cherished a secret love for Constance. The relative newcomers are Ben Griggs, a retired army general in his fifties, and his wife, Rose.

It is established at the outset that Ben Griggs is an intelligent, patient man trapped into marriage with a silly woman, and that Carrie and Mrs. Ellis are competing for influence over and attention from young Frederick. Carrie sees his tentative engagement to Sophie, Constance's young French niece, as a desirable alternative to Frederick's friendship with Payton, a writer of dubious talent and reputation. Constance is worried by the engagement, as the relationship is practical and devoid of romance. The wry observer of these human comedies is Ned Crossman, a loner who increasingly prefers the numbing company of drink to that of most of the people he knows.

Change enters their lives in the person of Nick Denery, a friend of their youth who had been engaged to Constance but jilted her to run away to become an artist. His anticipated return, with his wife, after more than twenty years has Constance in a state of excitement and fear. The irony is that Nick, too, is enmeshed in the toils of habit and pretense and, despite his wider experience of the world, has grown in wisdom and maturity even less than they have. Nick's arrival forces everyone to acknowledge both the passing of time and the person each has become in those years.

Sophie and Frederick are the two young people in the group. Sophie, who helps with the guests, is the daughter of Constance's brother, who married a French woman and died abroad during World War II. She is a spirited girl and much of her shyness is protective coloring in this strange land for which she never feels an affinity.[3] Sophie is a practical young woman who has agreed to a marriage of convenience with Frederick as an escape to greater independence and economic security. She likes Frederick, and, motherlike, tries to protect him, knowing he is dominated by his mother and grandmother and probably aware he is homosexual. Marriage to Frederick and living together comfortably as friends is not the dream of her heart, however, and as soon as a viable alternative presents itself, she seizes upon it.

That opportunity arises in act 3. Act 2 closes on Nick Denery making passes at her and then falling into a drunken stupor on her makeshift bed in the living room. She does not call for help but simply goes to sleep in a chair, since she does not see the situation as a threat to her reputation. In the morning in act 3, she learns that small-town 1949 Americans take a different view of her predicament. Mrs. Ellis tries to protect her and oust Nick, Rose is scandalized, and Constance is outraged, although she believes in Sophie's innocence. While Sophie thinks the American reaction ridiculous, she uses it to extort five thousand dollars from Nina Denery when she arrives to patch things up. As Jacob Adler points out, Sophie's successful blackmail attempt is prompted by the most original motive ever to grace the stage: the desire to be free of the obligation to be grateful. Although Nina offers the money as a gift, Sophie *insists* it be blackmail. She has no desire to "be friends" with Nina and refuses to be a "charity girl."[4] The Denery payoff permits her to do as she desires: forget about marrying Frederick and return to Europe.

Still in her teens, Sophie seems older and more clear eyed about life than Frederick and even Constance, Rose, and Carrie, women in their forties. Sophie's maturity results in part from her harsh life in France during the German occupation, and in part from her logical, rational mind. It is also the result of accepting personal responsibility for her life. It is Sophie who articulates the theme of *The Autumn Garden* in the conversation with Ned Crossman that closes act 1. He chides her about the choices she is making, particularly the folly of marrying Frederick. She answers that she is doing the best she can and suggests that perhaps the problem with Ned and the others is that they have not tried to do their best.[5] That simple statement encapsulates Hellman's central message, that it is one's responsibility to do the very best with one's life and talents, however modest these may be. It is not too late for people in their autumn years to assume responsibility, Hellman told Harry Gilroy of the *New York Times* (25 February 1951); the play does not imply that people cannot do anything about their empty lives: "It is meant to say the opposite—they can do a great deal with their lives."

While Sophie represents personal accountability in youth, Mrs. Mary Ellis, in the winter of her life, represents taking responsibility for oneself and completing one's life with honor. She, too, does not flinch from looking reality straight in the eye. Like Fanny Farrelly of *Watch on the Rhine,* Mary Ellis is one of Hellman's memorable forthright characters. Mrs. Ellis's sharp humor targets irritating, obnoxious behavior, as at the beginning of act 2, when Nick is making a pest of himself. She rebukes him, suggesting that he "try something intellectual for a change. . . . try to make a paper hat out of the newspaper or get yourself a nice long piece of string." Harold Clurman, who directed the play on Broadway, points out that Mrs. Ellis "doesn't crack jokes for the sake of fun."[6] The keynote of her character is honesty, a desire to keep things as straight as possible and not kid herself or others.

Mrs. Ellis loves Frederick but has no illusions about him. When Frederick's bland personality and meager experience become insufficient enticements for the man to whom he is drawn, Mrs. Ellis has anticipated this, realizing that it is Frederick's money that interests his friend. Her response to her daughter's righteous indignation at the possibility of her allowance being withheld is a typical Hellman aphorism: "There is no morality to money, Carrie, and it is immoral of people to think so." Mary Ellis's candor extends to herself as well; she knows her own limitations and is impervious to flattery. She explains her power over the family money: "One comes to be bored with those who fool themselves. I say to myself, one should have power, or give it over. But if one keeps it, it might as well be used, with as little mealymouthness as possible." In *Three* Hellman observes that most people, herself included, grow more practiced but not necessarily wiser with age (T 7–8). Mary Ellis, however, is a woman more "practiced about life and mischief," and who has achieved wisdom through honesty and courage.

Frederick Ellis is a pleasant young man with a mild sense of humor and a kind disposition. Despite his grandmother's efforts to stiffen his backbone, it is clear by act 3 that nothing is really changed for him. For a brief moment in act 2, when he defends his invitation to Payson to accompany them to Europe, Frederick speaks of the "wonderful things [there are] to see and learn about" and voices his longing to lead his own life. Before the speech is ended, his courage fails, and he pleads with his mother to let him go for just six months. It is a pathetic request, as his grandmother points out: "Sad to ask so little." His relationship with Sophie is gentle, kind, but slightly formal. The morning of the "scandal," he is easily persuaded to go to New Orleans without her, only protesting to the women, "You all seem to know what's right, what's best, so much faster than I do." His life is ruled by his mother's needs and demands; with no one else is he guaranteed a place of such supreme importance. It is also difficult to resist the comfortable, familiar patterns without the impetus of love to spur him on, and his feelings for Sophie are not sufficient motivation.

The person for whom Frederick is central is his mother, Carrie Ellis. She feels he is the only person of real value left for her in life, and in her great need, she almost always treats him inappropriately—at times as if he were a very young child, at others as if he were her lover, but never as an independent adult entitled to make his own decisions. Guided solely by that which is considered socially correct, she has cultivated no inner resources of her own; she lives a merely responsive life, adrift in the emotions and needs of the moment. Typically, she will blurt out her feelings, make rash threats or promises, and then repent and apologize. Carrie is a reasonably smart woman, but her anxiety renders her intelligence virtually useless. As Mrs. Ellis says to Frederick, even when his mother is right, "she talks and talks until she gets around to being wrong," a remark Hammett once made about Hellman (UW 244). At play's end, Carrie is just as she was; her moment of honesty departs, without effect, overridden by need. Her urge to protect Sophie is sincere but also fleeting. Now she and her son will drive off to New Orleans and all is well—all will be as it has been.

Rose Griggs is another woman in thrall to society's expectations of her, a woman her husband describes in act 1 as an "Army manual" wife. She has devoted her energies to being charming and decorative but now without the freshness of youth or the sparkle of intelligence to support them, her coquettish graces are merely tiresome. Rose is not very smart, nor does she feel the need to be. She does not bother to keep the simplest facts straight, speaking of her husband's fighting in the Pacific when, in fact, he fought in Europe. Such cavalier disregard for facts and for other people's feelings makes Rose's conversation a trial, and it is little wonder her husband yearns to divorce her.

For Rose, other people exist primarily as an audience to be dazzled by her charms, a mirror to reassure her that she herself exists. Ben complains in act 2 that Rose has "done more than stay young"; she has "stayed a child." Her clothes are too youthful, her psyche frozen in time. She cannot understand why Ben wants to divorce her and insists there must be another woman, the only reason that makes sense to her. The ploys she uses to dissuade Ben are grounded in fantasy: she tries to make him jealous; she pretends their sons would be devastated, when in fact they are, as their father describes them, "hard men to love," with little regard for their parents; she claims that Ben's long-dead mother would be horrified, when the truth is she thought Rose a poor choice of wife for her son.

Despite her irritating ways, there is a touching vulnerability in Rose. The doctor's diagnosis of serious heart trouble frightens her, and in act 3 she speaks to Ben honestly, admitting that neither her sons nor her brother will help her. She asks Ben to stay with her just one year and promises that at the end of that time she will give him a divorce. Ben agrees, and when she leaves to pack, there is the possibility that Rose may have changed significantly, freed from pretense and in touch with reality at last.

Ben Griggs is not so sanguine about their future together. He admits to Ned Crossman that he doesn't like Rose and expects to like her even less. Yet, once convinced that Rose's heart trouble is real, he responds with kindness and reassurance. In act 3, his choice to remain with Rose leaves him with shaking hands and the feeling that "there's no Benjamin Griggs." The dreams of starting a new life that he confided to Ned in act 1 must now be postponed indefinitely. There is the impression that his marriage has been a grievous mismatch of temperaments and intelligence, as well as a betrayal of his own essential nature.

Perhaps the most significant and universal speech in the play is Griggs's revelation in the third act that it is not just the big dramatic moments in life that count, but all the everyday experiences, too, that prepare one for them. Hellman had such a difficult time with this speech that Hammett took over and wrote the final version, in which Griggs realizes that "there are no big moments you can reach unless you've a pile of smaller moments to stand on. That big hour of decision . . . . it just doesn't come suddenly. You've trained yourself for it while you waited—or you've let it all run past you and frittered yourself away." Griggs believes that he has frittered himself away, and suspects that partly he is relieved that Rose's heart condition releases him from the responsibility of change. The future does not seem as bleak as it might for Ben and Rose, however. Their honesty with themselves and each other is a promising note on which to set forth, and suggests that, like Sophie and Mrs. Ellis, they will do the best they can and thereby restore integrity and worth to their lives.

The glamorous Denerys make their appearance late in act 1—Nick energetic and eager to see his friends; Nina attractive, chic, with little to do except wait around for Nick, smooth over his tactless remarks, and try to respond appropriately to the lies he improvises to flatter his friends. Hellman makes clear that the Denerys are enmeshed in well-worn patterns designed to bring a bit of drama to what are essentially wasted, empty lives. Nick periodically needs new people to charm, new hearts to conquer, deriving his sense of himself from his effect on people, much like Rose. But whereas Rose is an annoying prattler, Nick is a boor and a cad, and his efforts frequently end messily, with Nina left to clean up and make amends. Her dread of this homecoming as another disaster-bound episode proves justified by act 3. Nina is an intelligent, even witty, woman of wealth and breeding whose money they live on while maintaining the charade that Nick is an artist who earns sizable commissions. She finally tells him the truth about himself as an artist, that he is a "gifted amateur." For Nick, who lives on illusion and promoting illusion, this is a betrayal. Nina needs Nick to feed her self-contempt as she orbits him, like a satellite to his sun.

The range and variety of Nick's obnoxious behavior are displayed in act 2. The portrait he has bullied Constance into sitting for is as unflattering as possible, and he distracts her from the others' complaints about it by telling Constance that Ned admitted he has always loved her. Then he informs Carrie that her son has bought a ticket for his friend Payson to accompany them to Europe. Later, bored and drinking steadily, he tries to get Mrs. Ellis and Sophie to pay attention to him, but Mrs. Ellis fends him off with sharp remarks about how he constantly touches or leans on people: "One should have sensuality whole or not at all. . . . Don't you find pecking at it ungratifying?" The evening ends in a shambles, with his passing out on Sophie's bed. In most of Nick's interactions it is as if the other person is not real to him. He has no ability to empathize, to either imagine or care how his words or actions affect others; they are there only to gratify his whims, to supply him with temporary purpose, to reassure him that he exists.

But even Nick can stir pity in the heart of the observer. First, when he asks for Sophie's understanding because he is "old and sick." Then when he and Nina reconcile and he comes as close as he probably ever will to recognizing and accepting the truth about himself and their relationship. But within moments, he disparages his old friends as "damn bores, with empty lives" and launches gaily into plans for the good times ahead, and Nina happily cooperates. Their pattern is complete. He is once again her darling Nicky, sent off by train while she stays behind to make amends to Sophie. The young girl shrewdly perceives their pattern: "How would you and Mr. Denery go on living without such incidents as me? I have been able to give you a second, or a twentieth honeymoon."

Perhaps the most touching pair of characters is Constance Tuckerman and Ned Crossman, both of whom illustrate the point that "continually imagining what might have been allows us to avoid the need to do something constructive in the present, or build hopes for the future."[7] True to her name, Constance has devoted her inner life to dreams of Nick Denery returning for her someday. She is a pastel soul, gentle, soft, and delicate like the Renoir paintings she loves, at once "a dignified lady—and a little girl [who] idealizes or romanticizes everyone."[8] Fidelity to her genteel upbringing has cost her the full, active use of her intelligence, and her sexual maturity. References to her oblique, shuttered approach to life occur throughout the play, as in act 2, when Sophie tells her, "I think perhaps you worry sometimes in order that you should not think." Constance observes of Nick's portrait of her, "I don't look very bright," and then acknowledges, "Well, I haven't been very bright." Nick's homecoming, played out in her imagination in a hundred ways over the years, has forced her to abandon the veils of romance and see Nick as he is. Ned Crossman saves her from the lure of disillusionment and bitterness by pointing out that Nick never asked her to idealize him. She realizes that she knew all about Nick twenty-three years ago and chose to ignore the reality in favor of "sleeping with her dreams." The poignancy of the waste of her life is deepened by her humility in recognizing it. She now asks Ned to forgive her for "wasting all these years" and summons the courage to ask him to marry her.

Her simplicity and candor compel Ned to equal honesty. He has avoided taking responsibility for his life, using the excuse that everything would have been different if only Constance had returned his love. His failure to win her absolved him from further ambition and gave him license, as Ben Griggs points out, to deliberately waste his life.

Ned uses his humor to deflate "pretense, sham, foolishness," and his contempt for the foibles of others gratifies his pride and makes him feel he has a "little claim to wisdom."[9] He also uses it in the service of kindness, to smooth over an awkward patch or to make his shrewd but potentially painful insights more palatable. But as he admits to Constance, he has been "busy looking into other people's hearts so [he] wouldn't have to look into [his] own." In facing up to himself, Ned, too, apologizes for misleading Constance into thinking he was still in love with her, for fooling them both. Bereft of any illusions of superiority, he says, "I've never liked liars—least of all those who lie to themselves." And just as he has always helped her, Constance in turn helps him: "Never mind," she says. "Most of us lie to ourselves. Never mind."

The power of the play's ending lies in its very simplicity. Constance and Ned speak to each other from their hearts. They have more substance than they are aware of, built from their ability to care about others and their deep friendship for each other. Yet the fact remains that their lives exemplify "the failure of inaction."[10] Marvin Felheim contends that "the kind of drama we have in *The Autumn Garden* is the only kind which makes for modern tragedy." In this play Hellman attains the "artistic, poetic and moral" dimension of Chekhov.[11]

CHAPTER SIX

Toys in the Attic

Hellman's last original play explores the destructive aspects of sibling love and uncovers dark implications that have been stored and forgotten, like childhood toys in the attic. The opening of *Toys in the Attic* on 25 February 1960 provoked a storm of controversy not unusual for a Hellman play. Some reviewers charged that this was a steamy tale inspired by Tennessee Williams; kinder ones saw a Chekhov influence. Kenneth Tynan in *The New Yorker* saw it as "a treatise on abnormal psychology" and "an inquiry into the moral consequences of wealth" (5 March 1960). Katharine Lederer found the play "reflects Hellman's constant, lifelong concern with the necessity for self-knowledge and the disastrous effects of its absence. Love and money are only means of effecting an end made inevitable by these characters' beginnings."[1] William Saroyan, who accompanied Alice Griffin to the opening, told her as the curtain fell, "I wish I'd written that."

Hellman reports that Hammett had suggested to her a plot about a man whom others love and serve, desiring nothing for themselves but only success for him. When he succeeds, they withdraw their affection, and so he fails again. "I can write about men, but I can't write a play that centers on a man," she told him. "I've got to . . . make it about the women around him, his sisters, his bride, her mother" (P 206). While Julian Berniers is the focus of the women in the play, the audience is focused on two sets of women, paired primarily with each other: Julian's unmarried sisters, Anna and Carrie, and his childlike wife, Lily, and her mother, Albertine Prine.

The sets parallel each other in certain respects. Both team an older, rational, more intelligent woman capable of compassion for others with a younger, neurotic woman. Albertine, whose unexpected arrival at the sisters' modest New Orleans home precipitates the action, is a wealthy widow with a cool, enigmatic style that contrasts with that of her bizarre daughter and with self-effacing Anna and neurotic Carrie.

Used to money, appreciative of it, and realistic about what it can and cannot do, Albertine's mature view counterpoints Lily's and Julian's childishness. As the only wealthy person Julian knows, he turns to her as a mentor when he joins the ranks of the wealthy through a real-estate deal made possible by inside information supplied to him by a former lover. The long exchange between Julian and Albertine on the subject of money is the centerpiece of act 2. Julian is jubilant, so delighted to have the $150,000 that he puts cologne on it and asks Albertine if people like her think it's a lot of money. She answers, "People like me think it's a good beginning." When Julian boasts, "I know what I want and I'm going to be happy getting it," Albertine warns him that "it's not simple being happy, and money doesn't seem to have much to do with it, although it has to do with other things more serious."

In this act Julian reveals the self he has hidden from his sisters: he is childlike and vulnerable, his brashness a shield for wounded pride and lack of self-confidence, whereas in act 1 he seems insensitive and bullying with his sisters. The sympathy he earns in the scene with Albertine amplifies the impact of his downfall in act 3. In addition, Albertine, the one person genuinely pleased for his good fortune, points the way for the audience response. When Julian confides that the others seem upset by his gifts, Albertine says, "There's something sad in not liking what you wanted when you get it. And something strange, maybe even mean," confirming the impression that Carrie and Lily have not reacted normally, as well as foreshadowing the even stranger, meaner actions of act 3.

The thorn in Albertine's flesh is her daughter, Lily, whom Julian aptly calls his "infant bride" in act 1. "A frail, pretty girl of about twenty-one," Lily seems much younger. She is an appropriate choice for so unsuccessful a man as Julian, because a young woman thirteen years his junior would look up to him. "Considering his dependence upon his sisters," Lorena Holmin points out, "it is consistent that he would marry a woman with similarly possessive traits."[2] Lily resembles Carrie in that she is possessive, pretty, childish, and neurotic. Lily tells her mother in act 2: "I never wanted to have money. I hate money. You know that, Mama." She then gives a highly romanticized account of their living in a shabby Chicago hotel, cooking in the bathroom and giving Julian her share of meat "when he wasn't looking because he likes meat, and I was very happy." Her mother, impatient with Lily's naïveté, retorts: "How often the rich like to play at being poor. A nasty game, I've always thought . . . I don't think Julian would have liked the meat game for very long; and neither would you if the shortage had lasted much longer." But for Lily, poverty means feeling useful, needed, important, all very new, heady experiences for her.

Lily is so often idiosyncratic in speech and bizarre in behavior that the question arises whether she might be retarded or disturbed. Even she wonders. Near the end of act 3 she asks her mother if there is something the matter with her. Albertine is only just prevented from saying "yes" by Henry's warning gesture. Henry Simpson is Albertine's black chauffeur and lover, an alliance that puts them both in social peril. Her eccentricities, such as living at night and sleeping the days away, are adaptations to protect their relationship. "You haven't seen anybody in years, except Henry, of course," remarks Lily in act 2, revealing that Albertine has cut herself off from society. Despite Henry's kindness and concern, Lily resents him because he is the center of her mother's life.

Lily is so fearful of her mother's displeasure that she dithers when she speaks to her, provoking the very exasperation she hopes to avoid. This same fear surfaces in her marriage with Julian. She repeatedly asks Julian if he is angry with her, if she has done wrong, if she has done harm. The irony, of course, is that eventually she does do very grave harm. Lily is convinced that no one could possibly want her. In her marriage to Julian, in their sexual compatibility, she experiences a brief, joyous respite from this withering view of herself. Distraught when Julian is unable to make love to her and terrified that he plans to leave her, she asks her mother, "Did you sell me to Julian, Mama? . . . Did he marry me for money?" Although Albertine denies this, Lily is attuned to that which supports her inner terror, and this makes her a prime target for Carrie's manipulation.

Lily lives as her mother does and her society encourages, centering her life upon a man. However, her ability to love is limited, directed at filling the void that should be her self but is, instead, a great aching need to be loved. She looks to others for approval and fulfillment, and when Julian fails to pay attention to her, she behaves like a child, bruising herself, cutting herself, and lying to get his attention. Her need is so intense, so all-consuming, that she will sacrifice anything and anyone to satisfy it, demonstrating that a human being bereft of self-love is dangerous to herself and others.

The second set of women, Julian's sisters, Anna and Carrie, are loosely based on Hellman's paternal aunts, Hannah and Jenny, who, as she describes in *Maybe,*

> lived doing the uncomplaining work of women brought up by middle-class intellectual parents who grew more educated as they grew poorer; going out to find any kind of work in a social class where that was a kind of disgrace; certainly pained by it once upon a time, but not by the time I knew them; proud, cranky, married to each other; frightened of life with brave faces; never owning anything that didn't come from sales or cheap auctions. (M 76–77)

In a humorous recollection of their waiting upon her father and vying for his attention during the summer of his rheumatic attack, Hellman observes that "Without question both my aunts were in love with their brother" (M 80). However, sisterly affection is transformed in the play into a sinister force. As Tom Scanlon notes, Hellman "is at her best when presenting a well-made family war" as when she focuses on "the destructiveness of the family" in *Toys in the Attic.*[3]

The leisurely opening scene of the play details their lives together and delineates their characters. Although they are only four years apart in age, Anna acts like a mother to her siblings and seems older than forty-two. Carrie, like Lily, behaves as if she were far younger than she is. Their low-paying jobs as secretary and saleswoman add little to their lives, and without Julian life has lost its savor. They are oppressed by the heat and their lack of purpose and restless at the prospect of an empty future. Carrie continually looks to the past, to that happier time before Julian married, and Anna, who accepts the reality of his marriage, dreams that he and Lily will have a child and settle near them.

The idea of focusing on themselves is utterly foreign to them, as it was to most women of the fifties. They have long planned a trip to Europe, the funds for which repeatedly have been diverted to Julian, but, as in Chekhov's *Three Sisters,* they "only think they want to go."[4] Their unsought, unwelcome freedom seems to come too late. Both women fear the advance of middle age and speak as if they are already old. To Carrie's suggestion that they can save for another year to go to Europe, Anna replies, "A year is a long time—now." Carrie reflects that pink is no longer a good color for her, that she "kind of changed color" as she grew older. Each woman fears that her looks and her chances in life are fading away, but neither is ready to reassess her life and replace Julian as its center.

Anna has supported her brother and sister financially from the time she was twenty, when their father died, and her maternal responsibilities were assumed even earlier, at their mother's death. With no life outside of her family, she routinely puts the needs of others first. Throughout the play she is occupied with tasks of domestic service—cooking, serving, ironing—too busy caring for others to know what her own desires and goals are. When Julian expresses his heartfelt thanks for her generosity, she answers with her own gratitude: "You are our life. It is we who should thank you." But her role has its costs, too, and among them is her loneliness, to which Carrie is indifferent. Anna's attempts to fulfill her need for companionship through her sister and brother were doomed to only partial success, for Julian and Carrie are different from Anna in their tastes, interests, and abilities. When Carrie sneers at Anna's plans for a solitary trip to Europe, warning, "You will be lonely," Anna replies, "That's all right. I always have been." A mother-child relationship is not a relationship of peers and cannot satisfy needs outside its sphere.

Like any parent, surrogate or actual, Anna makes mistakes. Among the more serious is that she has failed to accept Julian as he actually is, and she and Carrie may have encouraged his irresponsibility by not letting him suffer the consequences of his actions. In regard to money, Anna appears to take a harder line toward Julian but actually indulges him as totally as, and perhaps more generously than, Carrie does. When they wait for Julian and Lily, Carrie cautions Anna not to be cold toward him. Anna defends herself: "Why do you so often make it seem as if I had been severe and unloving? I don't think it's true."

When their brother does arrive, the formulaic way Anna quizzes him and Carrie tries to "protect" him indicates that this scene has been enacted many times. His return, rich and gift laden, does not relieve the strain on their relationship; it exacerbates it. His presents are not to Anna's taste, but she dances with him in the evening coat he gave her while Carrie jeers that she looks "like a real fool." Anna's concern for his best interests prompts her to take his gifts seriously and thereby accept the reality of change. Her nonchalance about the loss of their jobs through Julian's intervention maddens Carrie, who snarls, "Well, you go to Europe and I'll go to work."

It is Anna who speaks the truth to Carrie. Carrie dares her to ask Julian if he was paid to marry Lily: "You used to tell us that when you love, truly love, you take your chances on being hated by speaking out the truth." Anna accepts the challenge, but it is Carrie, not Julian, whom she confronts: "All right. I'll take that chance now and tell you that you want to sleep with him and always have." She blames Carrie for driving Julian away: "This time I say he will go forever. You lusted and it showed. He doesn't know he saw it, but he did see it, and someday he'll know what he saw."

Anna is a woman who faces up to the present and the future, despite her fears. "I am a woman who has no place to go," she tells Carrie, "but I am going, and after a while I will ask myself why I took my mother's two children to be my own." Carrie, on the other hand, is characterized by Charles Walcutt as "a cluster of fears and frustrations and proprieties, with hardly any controlling 'self' apparent."[5] Alan Downer sees Carrie as "what evil must always be, the other side of good, tragic because she cannot know of her enslavement, because she can never have the opportunity to escape."[6]

From the opening moments of the play, as Carrie and Anna argue about leaving the plants outside with a storm coming, it is clear that Carrie's reasoning is a projection of her own feelings, an assumption that others, even plants, must react as she does. She invalidates others by ignoring their views, as when she insists, despite Anna's protests, that Anna likes their house. Carrie not only tells other people what they think but, she also acts upon her presumptions. When Carrie reveals to Anna that she sent Julian a thousand dollars out of their savings, she fends off Anna's objections: "But I knew you would want to send it." Carrie often adds Julian in to give weight to her opinions, to legitimize her behavior, or to present herself as the one most concerned about him, most sensitive to his needs, most in his confidence.

Before Julian arrives in scene 1, Carrie mentions his name twenty-nine times. But when he comes home, eager to share his good fortune, Carrie treats his gifts as insults: the fancy dresses are "whore's clothes." Carrie tries to hold time at bay; she fantasizes that when she wakes up "it will be years ago" in the past, when the prepubescent alliance with her brother allowed her, starved for love, to share in the favorite child's banquet. She and Julian frequently evoke their childhood through allusions, words, and rituals, as when they greet each other with Carrie jumping off the porch into his arms. When she learns of Julian's affair ten years earlier with Charlotte Warkins, Carrie denies this, insisting that Julian "was an innocent boy." Katherine Lederer believes that "Carrie can't accept Julian's having sexual relations with any woman, perhaps not so much because she wants him for herself but because the act makes Julian a man, not a boy."[7] This is consonant with Carrie's denial of her own sexuality and her emphasis on their preadolescence. Carrie's bitterness, resentment, and jealousy feed on Julian's failure, and she is enraged when he confides in Anna rather than in herself. She taunts Anna to find out if Julian married from choice: "Let's go and ask your darling child. Your favorite child, the child you made me work for, the child I lost my youth for."

Genial as Julian seems, he harbors resentments for past humiliations. His new wealth seems to open his eyes to the demeaning way Carrie treats him. When she is rude and domineering in act 1 he asks, "Did you always use that tone with me?" She virtually commands him to come inside in act 2, when he is with Albertine, but he protests that he is a "new man . . . You got to talk to me different now, like I'm a tycoon," believing that only wealth entitles one to respect and courtesy. And he refuses to apologize to her boss: "That's one of the things I don't ever have to do anymore. That's one of the things money's going to buy us all."

Carrie refuses even to try to change. She would hold Anna prisoner even though she says she no longer loves her. And then she gets her chance to force events to her will. Alone together, she and Lily are free to join in sabotaging Julian's success. In speaking of Carrie's decision to goad Lily into phoning Warkins and to supply the information that will result in Julian's being beaten and robbed, Walcutt says: "Here evil looks out of the frivolous void—strong, conscious, capable evil that plans and acts with shocking efficiency. By her frightful action Carrie defines and declares herself; she becomes responsible because she knows what she wants and plans how to get it, willing to hurt other people as much as is necessary to gain her end."[8]

Carrie greets the beaten Julian with smiles, purring words of encouragement, bustling off to prepare his favorite soup. Stunned, he asks, "You *like* me this way?" The audience knows the answer. The sad truth is that Carrie's sense of self-worth is predicated on her brother's diminished self-esteem. Carrie may believe that she has halted time and returned life to the form that best satisfies her, but the play is open ended. The movie version, which starred Wendy Hiller as Anna, Geraldine Page as Carrie, and Margaret Leighton as Albertine, leaves no doubts. Anna and Julian depart, with Carrie at the fence calling to them, pleading with them to return.

Toys in the Attic is "written with a firm hand and an understanding heart" and invites an examination of certain paths to self-fulfillment.[9] In addition to the dangers of self-deception, Hellman also illustrates the danger of martyrdom. The social expectation in the fifties, that women should live their lives for others, may have seemed noble, but it entailed hidden costs. Not the least is that in nourishing a sense of self on so meager a diet, what one develops may not be a beautiful character but a ravenous appetite, like Carrie's, to devour those one presumably loves.

CHAPTER SEVEN

An Unfinished Woman and *Pentimento*

An Unfinished Woman, which won the National Book Award for 1969, marks a departure for Lillian Hellman into an entirely new genre. Many critics were surprised that the memoir neither focused on the writer at work nor mined the rich vein of gossip anticipated in the life of someone who had worked more than thirty years in the theater. Instead, Hellman "presents her life . . . as process, including a number of diary entries," and expands the genre to include exploring memory in order to discover one's personal truth, an issue that Hellman acknowledges in the final paragraph as a lifelong preoccupation.[1] Readers also expected her to focus on a roster of celebrities, but the people she chose were those, ranging from the famous to the obscure, who had mattered most to her, who, by refraction, best revealed her to her self.

Perhaps the most daunting feature of a memoir is that it forces the writer to acknowledge that the past is indeed past, over with, finished. From the title to the last sentence, however, Hellman takes a defiant stance toward time. The title provoked considerable speculation. Some people read "unfinished" as "unvarnished," and others felt it meant that parts of her life were omitted and would be included in later memoirs. For Martha Gellhorn the word meant "inaccurate, untrustworthy." Timothy Adams suggests that "unfinished" may best be understood as incomplete in the sense that it is part of Hellman's ongoing effort to discover what she "meant by truth" and thereby to make sense of her life, a process she completes in *Maybe,* the last of her four memoirs (280).[2]

For all Hellman's desire to find the truth, there is an armored quality to this first attempt to make the private self public. Pamela Bromberg points out that "not surprisingly, Hellman in this first memoir is establishing for herself a public image that fits comfortably into the literary culture and mythology of her own era." That era was masculine-identified and Hellman's experiences in the Spanish civil war and in Russia during World War II "certify her credentials as a woman who could move anywhere in a man's world."[3]

Stylistically, *An Unfinished Woman* can be divided into three sections. The first, based in America, begins as a conventional autobiography and goes on as a bare-bones, chronologically organized, sometimes flippant account of her background, childhood, and young adulthood, up to and including her marriage to Arthur Kober and the start of her thirty-year relationship with Dashiell Hammett. The economy with which such subjects are dealt can be judged from the fact that these subjects total sixteen pages. Chapters 7 through 13 focus on Hellman's experiences in Europe, particularly Spain and the Soviet Union, with Paris and London figuring as way stations to these more important destinations. These chapters are longer, and chapter 8, on her visit to Spain during the Spanish civil war, the longest at thirty-three pages, is clearly the book's centerpiece. The writing in this section is less glossy, less resistant to penetration, the memories presented as scenes, one blending into the next, creating a cinematic effect. Chronology is no longer the organizing principle, and Hellman often shifts from past to present and back again. The last section consists of three titled chapters, each focusing on a person of particular importance to Hellman. Chronology is used flexibly, and this section anticipates the portrait approach of her second memoir, *Pentimento.*

Early memories concern a childhood spent half the year in New Orleans and half in New York City. When Hellman's father lost her mother's considerable dowry in an attempt to run his own business, the family thereafter spent six months of the year in New Orleans at his sisters' boardinghouse and the other six "shabby poor" in New York at the mercy of the Newhouse family's collective scorn (9). Life in the North was a grim sojourn among people dominated by money and ruthless in acquiring it. The humiliations attendant on her "poor relation" status made Hellman an angry child, created an ambivalence toward money veering between extravagance and exaggerated respect, and perhaps accounted for her sensitivity to social and economic injustice (5). In contrast, Hellman found life in the South among warm, funny, generous people who loved her a welcome respite. It was here she sensed that life would be difficult for someone of her temperament, and became aware of "the conflict which would haunt me, harm me, and benefit me the rest of my life: simply, the stubborn, relentless, driving desire to be alone as it came into conflict with the desire not to be alone when I wanted not to be" (12).

A series of rebellious incidents culminating in Hellman's running away from home heralds the advent of adolescence. After the escapade, she is found by her father, who resentfully apologizes. The adventure brings recognition of her new status, awareness of her power over her parents, and a lesson "more useful and more dangerous: if you are willing to take the punishment, you are halfway through the battle" (29).

Experiences that mark her entry into adulthood include attending New York University and her first affair, "a loveless arrangement" with a malicious young man. The affair was brief but, as she reveals in *Maybe,* had a negative effect on her for years afterward (32). In *An Unfinished Woman,* however, she glosses over her low self-esteem as part of the "cool currency of the time" (33).

Hellman had better luck with work, landing a lowly but enviable job with Horace Liveright's publishing firm, renowned for a roster of remarkable writers and frequent, lavish parties. According to Hellman, her job skills were unimpressive and she was almost fired when she misplaced an important manuscript. She was saved only by her cool demeanor during her pregnancy and abortion. She avoids personal revelation in discussing her short marriage to Kober, presenting her marital life in terms of briefly held minor jobs, her first encounter with Fascism in Europe, and her job as a manuscript reader for Metro-Goldwyn-Mayer writing "idiot-simple" reports for Louis B. Mayer (57).

She divorced Kober in 1932 and lived with Dashiell Hammett thereafter "on and off and then on again" for thirty years. In 1937, she accepted an invitation to attend the Moscow Theater Festival, although Hammett reminded her that her interest was in writing plays, not in the theater per se, and that the festival would probably bore her. In recounting her trip to Moscow, she mentions that she "had a four or five hour wait and a change of railroad stations" in Berlin; the details of that journey appear in the "Julia" section of *Pentimento* (80). Back in Paris, a friend persuaded her to visit Spain; although, as she points out, "it didn't take much persuasion: I had strong convictions about the Spanish war, about Fascism-Nazism, strong enough to push just below the surface my fear of the danger of war" (82).

Those who, like Martha Gellhorn in 1981, suggest Hellman fabricated her Spanish civil war experiences, and could do so with impunity because all the other witnesses to the war were dead, overlook the fact that the memoir material appeared in *The New Republic* in 1938 as well as in *This Is My Best* in 1942.[4] Hellman's account of her trip to Spain is a highly personal, impressionistic series of diary entries that begin in Valencia 13 October 1937. In the course of her stay, she made a radio broadcast from Madrid and witnessed her first air raid in Valencia. In a cinematic account of her first air raid, as fear and confusion escalate, the action takes on the surreal qualities of a nightmare, rendered through increasingly distorted perceptions. Her grief and anger at America's failure to intervene was later channeled into *Watch on the Rhine* and *The Searching Wind*.

Her experiences in Spain left her feeling at odds with normal life; Paris depressed her, and London proved little better. The indifference to Spain evinced by members of the English upper class she met at a dinner party so incensed Hellman that she stormed out and fell and broke her ankle. During the enforced rest this entailed, she read Marx, Engels, Lenin, Saint-Simon, Hegel, and Feuerbach and found many of their ideas sympathetic. But unlike Hammett, who was committed to socialism and whose ability to be so made her at once "respectful, envious and angry," she could not make such a commitment, explaining that "rebels seldom make good revolutionaries, perhaps because organized action, even union with other people, is not possible for them" (118–19).

Once the United States entered World War II, Hammett enlisted, although he was forty-five. Hellman envied his ability to take "a modest road to what he wanted" and considered her own activities in support of the war effort—writing and making speeches—to be "idle lady stuff" (121). Relief came as an invitation to visit the Soviet Union on a cultural mission, offered, Hellman surmises, because of her pro-Soviet film, *The North Star.*

Invited to the Russian front, Hellman traveled to Lublin and then to Maidanek, a concentration camp recently taken from the Germans. Hellman alternates surreal, nightmare images of drowning, "covered with slime, pieces of me floating near my hands," with solid details of touching a pair of red shoes among "thousands . . . arranged by size and color," of death ovens, "large for men and women, small for children," of trenches filled "with human bones" to convey the overwhelming horror of the experience (153–54). She later declined the Russians' invitation to accompany them to the Polish front and then on to Berlin, aware that she lacked the courage and stamina to do so. A few weeks later in Moscow, she listened with joy and a fleeting pang of regret to the guns saluting the Russian capture of Warsaw.

Twenty-two years later Hellman revisited the Soviet Union, reconnecting with lost portions of her life, wondering, "Did other people do this, drop the past in a used car lot and leave it for so long that one couldn't even remember the name of the road?" (170) Chapters 12 and 13 form a spiral, circling in on the present, the recent past, the long past, times, places, people shifting, releasing memories as the narrative brushes past. The section opens as her plane approaches Moscow. Shocked to find herself crying, she recognizes that her tears "had to do with age and the woman who could survive hardships then and knew she couldn't anymore" (167).

Dreams of her beloved farm, sold in 1952 so that she and Hammett could survive, urge her to come to terms with this long-buried loss. Finally she acknowledges that that place, that time, that woman she once was are gone. A visit to the Writers' Union to collect royalties brings Hellman into conflict with an official who insists she count out the bundles of rubles owed her. Hellman refuses, saying, "I like what money buys, but I don't like handling it, and won't, and that's that" (175).

Chapter 13 shifts to the immediate past and opens on a deceptively quiet note. In Paris, just before she comes to Moscow, she goes on an excursion into the countryside with a man who has long been important to her, and she, delighted with his company, feels "young again on this journey that was his idea" (190). However, when he announces that he may soon marry, the idyllic mood is shattered and Hellman leaves for Budapest the next day, wracked by rage and self-doubt. She wonders, "Is it age, or was it always my nature, to take a bad time, block out the good times, until any success became an accident and failure seemed the only truth?" and it is a question worth asking in view of the unheroic light she casts herself in throughout the memoir (191).

The closest she comes to addressing what Bromberg sees as her "central, continuing conflict (both as subject and biographer) about her identity and achievement as a woman in a man's world" is when she asks herself why, "after the first failure, I had been so frightened of marriage, who the hell did I think I was alone in a world where women don't have much safety" (191). But she dismisses these thoughts as adolescent maunderings "without fully recognizing," believes Bromberg, the "conflict as a problem requiring analysis."[5] Memories of life with Hammett counterpoint her adventures in Budapest and Moscow, as if revisiting Europe throws the American portions of her life into relief and shows her what is most essential.

The final section of three profiles begins with Dorothy Parker. Hellman's relationship with Parker began inauspiciously at a party in 1931, at the height of Hammett's fame, with Hellman as "an unknown young woman among the famous" (212). She met Parker again in 1935 in Hollywood, and from then until Parker's death in 1967 they enjoyed a friendship unmarred by "a quarrel, or even a mild, unpleasant word" (213).

The next chapter, ostensibly a portrait of Helen, her housekeeper and companion for many years, is equally a portrait of Sophronia, who raised Hellman. Her memories of "these two black women [she] loved more than [she] loved any other women" begin with water images and dreams, symbols of the deepest levels of being (230). To her, they were "one person," her "mother," her source of self, and dreams of them are "a deep time-warning of my own age and death" (231). The heart of the chapter is the paradox of black-white relations: no matter how kind or loving some white people are, there is no forgetting all of those who are not. Hellman realizes that her love for these women does not place her in a category superior to most white liberals. There was much Sophronia and Helen did not, could not, share, much in their lives she knew nothing about, and theirs is, of necessity, an "unfinished" portrait.

The last portrait is of Dashiell Hammett, Hellman's "closest, most beloved friend" (256). Biography is not her intent, so she only sketches in his lifelong struggle with illness, his Pinkerton years which radicalized his political beliefs and provided the material for his detective fiction. When they met, he "was the hottest thing in Hollywood and New York," having written four of his major novels (260). Hammett's strict discipline while writing, his "care for every word," became Hellman's model for her own writing (270). This vital relationship "with its many interruptions but fundamental loyalty gave her the intimacy and emotional security she needed" so it is not surprising that the chapter is the richest, most fluid of the memoir.[6] Once free of biography's constraints, memories flow "out of order and out of time," diary entries merge with narrative, all the stories and thoughts of Hammett that permeate the previous chapters seem to add their force to this final loving tribute (259). Hellman's ultimate effect is a defiance of time, of death, suggesting yet another meaning of "unfinished," and reminding the reader that each life is a work in progress, that until one's last breath the not-so-final word is "However" (280).

Pentimento

The title of this 1973 "Book of Portraits," explains Hellman in a prefatory note, is a term used in art to describe the effect created when a painter viewed his work, then "repented" or "changed his mind," and painted over his first effort; years later, when the paint is old, one might see the original work, perhaps a tree showing through a dress or a dog through a child: "The old conception, replaced by a later choice, is a way of seeing and then seeing again." Looking back, Hellman notes, "I wanted to see what was there for me once, what is there for me now." In *Three,* she describes her treatment of time as "a kind of free association." Her chosen subject was not "what had been most important to me, but what had some root that I had never traced before" (T 586).

Her mission is exploratory: painting a series of portraits in the present to reveal a significance for her that may have been obscured in the past. Just as a portrait differs from a photograph by representing the artist's perception of the subject, so *Pentimento* is impressionistic: a transformation of nature and persons into the artist's personal vision of them. As a genre, autobiographical memoirs combine "historical self-explanation, philosophical self-scrutiny, [and] poetic self-expression."[7] Hellman's moral outlook is also characteristic of the genre.[8]

In choosing to write about others, Hellman reveals herself as well as her subject. Women's life-writing, as differentiated from men's, observes Mary G. Mason, delineates the self by relating it to others: "Lillian Hellman reveals most about herself . . . when she creates portraits of other people in her life."[9]

Hellman writes about "the people she loved and admired, the chosen others who reveal indirectly the chosen self."[10]

On Hellman's journey from childhood to maturity, the root she traces invariably grows into an aspect of love. The five portraits, presented in roughly chronological order, begin with sensual immigrant Bethe and Lillian as a child; followed by Uncle Willy, on whom she has a teenage crush; then beloved friend Julia; then Arthur Cowan, who wishes and does not wish to marry celebrity Hellman; and end with "Turtle," a recollection of Dashiell Hammett. A short coda sketches her mourning for him.

Hammett combines all the individual manifestations of love. People and places recalled lead inevitably to him, whether he is solving a predicament, as in "Cowan," judging Willy, or suggesting (in bed) the Bethe story can wait. It might be noted that even Hellman's method is attributable to that of the former Pinkerton man and detective-story writer: all the evidence is assembled piecemeal, and when it is fitted into place, a complete picture emerges.

In "Bethe" young Lillian sees "what I had never seen before"— sexual passion openly expressed between a man and a woman—and learns a truth about which, in later life, she challenges Bethe. Heavy-set, auburn-haired Bethe is a cousin brought from Germany for an arranged marriage but living with an Italian gangster. One day in a restaurant with Bethe, Lillian sees the man at another table and observes their silent, rhythmic movements. The confused young girl rushes away (28). Years later she remembers this scene as she dresses for her wedding to Arthur Kober. When Hellman goes to New Orleans to tell her aunts about her divorce from Kober, she again tracks down Bethe, now living with a plumber on the out-skirts of town. As Bethe tries to cover her naked body, Hellman makes her accusation: "It was you who did it. I would not have found it without you. Now what good is it, tell me that?" (47). "One drunken night I did try to tell Hammett about Bethe, and got angry when he said he didn't understand what I meant when I kept repeating that Bethe had had a lot to do with him and me" (48–49).

"Willy" is married to Hellman's great aunt Lily. Willy's veering fortunes are declared by great uncle Jake to be "a sign of a nation more interested in charm than in stability, the road to the end" (57). Larger than life in all aspects—build, vitality, position, friends, sports, sex—Willy is viewed as heroic by fourteen-year-old Lillian. "And I had other feelings for him, although I didn't know about them for years after the time of which I speak" (67).

Willy rose from dock worker to vice president of a "giant corporation" doing business in Central America. Gaps in the inquisitive girl's interest in Willy are filled in by Caroline Ducky, who, reports Hellman, had been "born into slavery in my mother's family and, to my angry eyes, didn't seem to want to leave it" (55). Caroline is the constant thread as the story is woven together, moving from past to present to near-present to past.

Years later, after a quarrel with Hammett, Hellman is in New Orleans, where she sees Willy. "He was much older: the large body hung now with loose flesh, the hair was tumbled, the heavy face lined and colored sick" (93). He drives her to a plan-tation house set in strawberry fields and says he will give the place to her, then confesses that he is broke. Suddenly transformed, he says he is going to Central America in a few days to begin a new climb to success and invites Hellman to accompany him. The myth of Uncle Willy still prevails with Hellman, who phones Hammett. He returns her to a reality she has refused to face and she returns to Los Angeles that night (97–98).

As Lillian progresses from awed child to smitten teenager experiencing "the struggles caused by love" to grown woman accepting an invitation from a downfallen hero, she evaluates her reactions then and now, sharing emotions both personal and universal. Relating the bayou trip with Willy, who leaves her for a "Cajun girl," older Hellman confides that since that first time of falling in love, "the mixture of ecstasy as it clashed with criticism of myself and the man was to be repeated all my life." As a mature woman she recognizes what she could not at the time: "the blindness of a young girl trying to make simple sexual desire into something more complex, more poetic, more unreachable" (75–76).

"Julia" is the most dramatic portrait, hinting immediately at mystery when Hellman says she has had to change the names because some of the principals are still alive, including Julia's mother, "perhaps" Julia's daughter, and "almost certainly" the daughter's father.

The emotional impact of this account was demonstrated during a television interview when Hellman was reading from the "Julia" chapter and broke down in tears: "I had written 'Julia' with enormous difficulty . . . . It was the most shocking thing that ever happened to me in public. Verbalizing your own words—something triggers emotions you can hide when you're at the typewriter."[11]

Appearing halfway in the five portraits, "Julia" relates the story of a memorable woman, Hellman's "beloved childhood friend." Central to the story is the train trip, an appropriate metaphor for the emotional journey. Train changes signal a new direction in the narrative, as the voyage which frames the story links three major incidents: the dangerous trip itself from Paris to Berlin; an earlier visit to Vienna, where Julia is hospitalized; and the meeting with Julia in Berlin.

Time moves from past to present and back again. The story begins in 1937, with Hellman to visit her friend Julia, a medical student in Vienna. Julia instructs Lillian to travel instead to Berlin: to carry to their anti-Nazi group in Berlin fifty thousand dollars to be used as bribes to free jailed political prisoners. Hellman reminisces about Julia.

Schoolmates at the age of twelve, Julia and Lillian spend weekends together at the mansion of Julia's grandparents. Julia's intelligence, beauty, and spirit are delineated from the point of view of her devoted friend. Then the narrative suddenly advances "almost twenty" years, and the reader is jolted as if the train had suddenly stopped: Julia is dead, and the time is the present. Hellman recounts that "I leaned down in a London funeral parlor to kiss the battered face that had been so hideously put back together" (114).

Remembrances return to the past. In Paris in 1934, unable to contact Julia in Vienna, Hellman reads of an attack on Socialists there by government troops and local Nazis. A telephone call from Vienna tells Lillian that Julia is in the hospital. Hellman travels to the hospital, but Julia, bandaged and immobile, cannot speak, can only touch Lillian's hand, and the women clasp hands. Waiting, Lillian falls asleep; when she awakes, Julia's bed is gone. In New York *The Children's Hour* opens and is a success. Julia writes to say she has had a baby and named it Lilly.

The final meeting in Berlin is told in Hellman's best narrative style; while the dialogue is restrained and unsentimental, an atmosphere of urgency and danger surrounds the action. Julia is waiting in the restaurant. "I went toward her with tears that I couldn't stop because I saw two crutches lying next to her and now knew what I had never wanted to know before" (137). Julia takes her hand and says that everything has gone fine; she plans to come to New York soon. The money, she says, which is hers, can save five hundred people, perhaps a thousand.

On 23 May 1938 a cable arrives from London saying that Julia has been killed and her body is at a funeral home. There a note awaits Hellman: after the Nazis found Julia in Frankfurt, her friends brought her to London, hoping to save her. It is signed "John Watson." Hellman is unable to locate him or the doctor. She returns to the United States with the body and, after Julia's family refuses all contact, has it cremated. In *Three,* Hellman adds that she had heard recently from London that when the Germans invaded, the couple who were boarding the baby, and the baby, were killed (T 452).

Almost certainly Julia is idealized by Hellman. She may be the ultimate embodiment of good that Hellman contrasted with evil throughout her life and writing career. In *An Unfinished Woman* Hellman refers to her Marxist friend Alice, who attended medical school in Vienna and was killed by the Nazis. It is not known to what extent Alice-Julia and the mission itself, although known to others at the time, were altered and enlarged upon.

When *Pentimento* was published in 1973, it was well received, as was the 1977 Academy Award–winning movie *Julia,* with Jane Fonda as Hellman and Vanessa Redgrave as Julia. But in 1980 and 1981 Hellman's account was attacked by Mary McCarthy and Martha Gellhorn, who charged that Julia was fictitious. In his biography of Hellman, Carl Rollyson details the "Julia" controversy.[12] "Through the second half of the seventies, Hellman's growing legend rankled people like Mary McCarthy—an anti-Stalinist since the 1930s who had for years detested Hellman's politics and writing," says Rollyson. Appearing on the Dick Cavett show on the Public Broadcasting System (PBS) on 25 January 1980, McCarthy stated that Hellman was an overrated writer and that everything she wrote was a lie, including "and" and "the." Hellman promptly brought a libel suit against McCarthy, Cavett, and PBS but died before the case came to trial.[13]

In January 1981 an essay appeared in *Paris Review* by Martha Gellhorn, third wife of Ernest Hemingway, who had been with him in Spain forty-four years earlier during the civil war. Gellhorn says that because she has been unable to make dates and facts match in "this wearisome effort," she also has questions "even about 'Julia.'"[14]

In 1983 Dr. Muriel Gardiner's autobiography was published. She had been an American medical student in Vienna and worked in the anti-Fascist underground. Rollyson reports that Stephen Spender, who had had an affair with Gardiner, was sure that Hellman's Julia was Gardiner. In June 1984,

Samuel McCracken's "'Julia' and Other Fictions by Lillian Hellman" appeared in *Commentary*. He repeats the charges made by McCarthy and checks and enlarges on the time schedule being incomprehensible.[15] Rollyson concludes the section on the Julia controversy by observing:

> Until readers begin to look for such things, discrepancies in dates, minor characters who are killed off and get renamed as major characters, are not usually noticed. Hellman herself may not have noticed, since she—like many of her readers—passionately identifies with the story she has to tell. For readers like [Bernard] Dick who see Julia as central to all of Hellman's work—as I do— the fictionalizing that assuredly took place seems less important than the artistic and biographical truth that for Lillian Hellman, Julia was real.[16]

If the atmosphere of "Julia" is one of tension, the impression of "Arthur W. A. Cowan" is one of excess, a crowd of details about "a man of unnecessary things." A wealthy, eccentric Philadelphia lawyer addicted to steaks, fast cars, and celebrities, Cowan is only partly understood by Hellman during their friendship. After his death she attempts to fathom the character of this unusual man.

Hellman was forty-eight and famous when they met, and he instantly fancied himself a suitor, although she considers him a friend. He is showy, temperamental, impetuous, reactionary, and generous. At the time, she responded with pleasure, irritation, or pain to Cowan's antics, but "seeing again" in the present, she realizes: "I was what he wanted to want, did not want, could not ever want, and that must have put an end to an old dream about the kind of life that he would never have because he didn't really want it. We have all done that about somebody, or place, or work, and it's a sad day when you find out that it's not accident or time or fortune but just yourself that kept things from you" (237).

In Hellman's portrait of Cowan, an attractive surface conceals a complex and troubled individual in whom "the need for recognition and approval is insatiable."[17] But Cowan's charm almost always rescues him from his fits of temper. The fast, expensive car, symbol of a man always on the move, is the cause of his death on a road in Spain. The details are mysterious.

"Turtle," a story about Hammett, takes place in the spring of 1940 at the Pleasantville farm. Hammett traps a large snapping turtle, which he shoots and then partially beheads, but the next morning it is still wandering around. It is apparent that the turtle symbolizes Hammett (266). In the present, Hellman appreciates his acceptance and will to survive: "He was prepared for the trouble and the sickness he had, and was able to bear it . . . with enormous courage, and quietness."[18]

Dashiell Hammett, as Hellman re-creates him here and in the other memoirs, is the "cool teacher" she sought as a young woman. The portrait is Hellman's perception of Hammett, painted by a woman who loved him. His drunkenness is never alcoholism, but rather the "fashionable" drunkenness featured in movies of the time, like *The Thin Man*. His womanizing is glamorized, as are their quarrels. There is no mention that he nearly died of syphilis. On the other hand, his dialogue is very much like that of his letters and of Nick Charles: debonair, witty, succinct, sometimes teasing, often exasperated. The characteristics Hellman delineates are not exaggerated. Hammett is intelligent and well rounded: his reading is prodigious, his writing engrossing, his woodland skills impressive. Above all, he is a man of principle and honor.

A final brief epilogue, "Pentimento" recounts Hellman's mourning shortly after Hammett's death and her acquaintance with a young black student she meets in 1961 at Harvard, where she is teaching writing. In Cambridge with her housekeeper, Helen, their rooms overlook the nursing home where Hammett would have stayed had he not died a few weeks earlier. Unable to sleep one night, Hellman goes to stand in front of the nursing home. This becomes a habit, and two or three nights a week she stands before the house until she is too cold to stay. As the term ends and she prepares to leave, she walks to the nursing home and remains for a long time. When she turns to go, the student, Jimsie, is there. "We didn't speak until I heard myself say, 'Pentimento.'" At a recent meeting Hellman remarks that it is too late for him to tell Helen, now dead, of his love for her. "I told it to her," he says, "the night I looked up your word, pentimento" (297).

CHAPTER EIGHT

Scoundrel Time

The dramatic core of *Scoundrel Time,* published in 1976, is Lillian Hellman's appearance before the House Un-American Activities Committee on 21 May 1952. She had tried twice before to write about the event: "I had strange hangups and they are always hard to explain. Now I tell myself that if I face them, maybe I can manage" (39). In this third book of memoirs, the narration draws upon devices of the drama, the suspense rising to a climax at the committee hearing. Proceeding episodically, *Scoundrel Time* concludes in 1953 with a spy-thriller experience, implying that the waves stirred up by the investigations are still breaking on faraway shores. Interspersed with the dramatic narrative is satire that is both humorous and biting, verbal cartoons that include Joseph McCarthy with nightmares revealing sexual proclivities, and his young henchmen Cohn and Schine as romping schoolboys.

The emotional atmosphere is one of fear, enhanced by Hellman's realistic details: fear of jail and rats, fear of blacklisting, fear of the future when the money runs out. The overwhelming climate of fear unleashed by the power of the committee seems as inexplicable today as it seemed 20 years after her hearing, when Hellman told students they were fortunate to be free from the atmosphere of fear that pervaded the fifties. Hellman borrows from the drama her technique of contrasts, emphasizing the wide divergences, in the time of the scoundrels, between decency and scurrility, directness and evasiveness, luxury and frugality, courage and fear.

Dashiell Hammett, the constant thread in the memoirs, appears as commentator and adviser, worried that Hellman might go to jail. He had recently been released after serving six months for refusing to disclose to HUAC the names of contributors to a bail fund for those HUAC accused.[1] In her "seeing again" mode, Hellman probes Hammett's radicalism: As a detective for Pinkerton, notorious for their strike-breaking, he had been offered five thousand dollars to kill a union organizer, later found lynched. Hellman feels that Hammett "in time . . . came to the conclusion that nothing less than a revolution could wipe out the corruption" (50).

Fearing that Hellman might display a characteristic anger to the committee, Hammett is against the course recommended by lawyers Joseph Rauh and Abe Fortas. They believe that the time is right for someone to take a "moral position" before the committee, to consent to discuss one's own life but to refuse to name others. Against Hammett's advice, Hellman agrees to do so.

As in drama, the episodes preceding the climax build suspense. Writer Clifford Odets and, later, director Elia Kazan invite her to meet when they are summoned by the committee. The Odets encounter she reports with restaurant setting, dialogue, and stage directions. When the waiter arrives, "Clifford put his finger to his mouth to shush me and began to whistle until the waiter went away." Suddenly Odets pounds on the table, spilling the wine, and yells out a prepared speech, telling off the committee. Later, at Odets's hearing, he "apologized for his old beliefs and identified many of his old friends as Communists" (66–69).

Elia Kazan's conversation is so roundabout, Hellman excuses herself, phones producer Kermit Bloomgarden, and learns that Kazan is trying to tell her that he plans to be a "friendly" witness and name his former friends as Communists, so that he can continue to work in Hollywood. Using "free association," Hellman's recollection of Kazan leads to earlier threats by film tycoons. Harry Cohn offers Hellman a contract to write and produce four movies of her own choice. Before signing the contract she is told she must compose and sign an oath that "nothing that you believed, or acted upon, or contributed to, or associated with could be different from what the studio would allow" (77). Her refusal to provide such a letter results in her being prevented from writing Hollywood screenplays, even of her own dramas. The movie version of *Another Part of the Forest* (1948) was the first casualty, a poor adaptation by Vladimir Pozner.

The stage is set for the climactic scene, beginning with the "tough spring" of 1952. Hammett is out of jail but penniless, as the Internal Revenue Service has attached his present and future income to pay his back taxes. After Hellman receives the subpoena, she and Rauh compose a letter dated 19 May 1952 to John S. Wood, chairman of the House Un-American Activities Committee. The letter acquired a life of its own, starring in three plays—*Lillian,* a one-woman show by William Luce, *Cakewalk* by Peter Feibleman, and *Are You Now or Have You Ever Been* by Eric Bentley. Bentley ("no friend of American drama, or of Hellman," notes Katherine Lederer) had been one of the attackers of the 1952 revival of *The Children's Hour,* which he claimed in the *New Republic* (5 January 1953) had been rewritten as an apologia for accused Communists.[2] (A close examination of the versions of 1934 and 1952 shows no substantial revisions.) In 1978–79 Bentley's play gained fame and profit by including, over Hellman's objections, the entire letter, which was read by famous guest actresses.

Five days before her hearing Hellman goes to Washington and fills the tense time with walking, eating out, and shopping for a hat, white kid gloves, and an expensive Balmain dress for the hearing: "It will make me feel better to wear it" (100). Reporting to Rauh's office the morning of the hearing, Hellman finds Rauh on the phone talking with the distinguished jurist Thurman Arnold. Arnold believes that Rauh and Fortas "are making a martyr of this woman" and that she should withdraw the letter. Hellman refuses to do so (106).

The letter had a powerful impact in its time, representing as it did one person's view that "to hurt innocent people whom I knew many years ago in order to save myself is, to me, inhuman and indecent and dishonorable." Hellman draws upon an image from dressmaking: "I cannot and will not cut my conscience to fit this year's fashions, even though I long ago came to the conclusion that I was not a political person and could have no comfortable place in any political group."

She was raised, the letter continues, "in an old-fashioned American tradition and there were certain homely things that were taught to me: to try to tell the truth, not to bear false witness, not to harm my neighbor, to be loyal to my country, and so on." She believes, she says, that the committee will "agree with these simple rules of human decency and will not expect me to violate the good American tradition from which they spring." She offers to tell the committee anything they ask about her "views or actions" if they will "refrain from asking me to name other people."³ If they agree to do so, she will waive her privilege against self-incrimination and not claim the protection of the Fifth Amendment. The committee replied by letter on 20 May, rejecting her offer.

As the hearing begins, committee counsel Frank Tavenner asks whether Hellman knew Martin Berkeley (a "lavish" witness), who claimed she was at a meeting of Communists in Hollywood in the summer of 1937 when actually she had been in Spain. Hellman refers to her letter and requests that the committee reconsider the offer she made in it.

Chairman John Wood instructs Tavenner to put into the record Hellman's letter and the committee's reply. Tavenner does so. Rauh springs to his feet and distributes copies of Hellman's letter to the press. When they finish reading her letter, a loud voice rings out from the press gallery: "Thank God somebody finally had the guts to do it" (113–14). There are no further questions, and an hour and seven minutes after it began, her hearing is over. Rauh believed the committee might have made a legal mistake in putting Hellman's letter into the record, and preferred to end the hearing rather than tangle with the situation they had created.

Although Hellman survives the hearing, just as Hammett survived jail, their life changes. Neither is able to work because of the blacklist. Their money dwindles. The farm is sold, and they agree to leave within a month.

Hellman goes to Rome to write for Alexander Korda a film adaptation of *The Blessing,* a novel by Nancy Mitford "that I would never have touched in the good days, hoping that I wouldn't always have to earn a living doing what I didn't like" (143). One day she is greeted by acquaintances Dick, a freelance CIA informant, and his wife, Betty (whose names Hellman has changed). Soon after, Hellman reads in the *Rome Daily American* that Senator McCarthy has issued a subpoena for her to appear before his committee. She telephones Hammett and learns there is no word of a subpoena. When she tells him of receiving a mysterious phone call, he instructs her to tip workers at her hotel to learn if someone has been inquiring about her. She discovers it is Dick. Years later she learns from a friend that Dick is no longer a CIA stringer because his wife was ashamed of that connection. But Betty is "still a valuable and highly paid [CIA] agent" (155–56).

The prose of *Scoundrel Time* continues and refines the unique style of the earlier two memoirs, an endless flow moving back and forth in time, as rhythmic as the sea Hellman loved. Descendants of the sharp dialogue that characterizes Hellman's plays are the memorable aphorisms in *Scoundrel Time,* like her echo of Voltaire: "Since when do you have to agree with people to defend them from injustice?" Dialogue abounds, whether it is questions from the committee, haranguing by Clifford Odets, or advice from Hammett, who has all the best lines.

The foolish, irrational behavior of the scoundrels makes them a likely target for Hellman's satire, which reveals the comic as well as the threatening aspect of the trio of McCarthy, Cohn, and Schine in this "sad, comic, miserable time of our history."

A good cook, and coauthor of a cookbook, Hellman again bases some of her best imagery on food, effectively contrasting destructive danger with homely, nourishing meals. The idea of Communists taking over the movies she reduces to the absurd in a food image comparing panicky film barons to peasants attacked by Cossacks in pre-Communist Russia: "It would not have been possible in Russia or Poland, but it was possible here to offer the Cossacks a bowl of chicken soup. And the Cossacks in Washington were now riding so fast and hard that the soup had to have double strength and be handed up by running millionaire waiters" (72).

Each of the memoirs is a learning experience for Hellman. In *Scoundrel Time* Hammett already knows what she will come to realize: not to depend on supposed friends to come to the rescue when she is in trouble; they are all "stinkers," he warns, who are not "going to pay any attention to your high-class morals" (59). It is a bitter lesson. She expected nothing better from McCarthy and his crew, but directs savage indignation at liberals who during those times stood by and did nothing. As Arthur Miller would observe many years later in discussing his reasons for writing *The Crucible:* "I was motivated in some great part by the paralysis that had set in among many liberals."[4] "So few people fought, so few people spoke out. I think I was more surprised by that than I was by McCarthy,"[5] stated Hellman.

Attacks and defenses in the reviews of the book are about evenly divided in the 110 "Writings about Hellman" in Mark W. Estrin's bibliography for 1976, the year of *Scoundrel Time*'s publication, and in the 129 items in 1977.[6] In the two publications Hellman criticized for their inaction, William Phillips in *Partisan Review* declared the book inaccurate, and Nathan Glazer in *Commentary* attacked Hellman for "finding no justification for public concern with communism" and for ignoring the "communist enemy."[7] William F. Buckley asked in the *National Review,* "What does one . . . say about a book so disorderly, so tasteless, guileful, self-enraptured?"[8]

Timothy Dow Adams believed that as a memoir *Scoundrel Time* is entitled "to embody [its] own moral vision of the past."[9] In the *New York Times* book review section of 25 April 1976, page 1, Maureen Howard compared *Scoundrel Time* to Emerson's *The American Scholar* as a fine moral essay. Robert Sherrill in the *Nation* noted a "sense of humor and a miraculous sense of perspective," a reminder "that people we assume to be allies can turn out to be treacherous indeed."[10]

CHAPTER NINE

Maybe

Maybe (1980) is unique among Hellman's memoirs. Free association no longer introduces a change of direction, as in the earlier three. In *Maybe* characters flit in and out as in a dream, in incidents that are clear-cut in themselves but enveloped in a mist of uncertainty. Time, formerly used elliptically to recount the past while commenting in the present, now doubles back on itself, like memory trying to recall a picture that is incomplete; some of the missing fragments appear later. The central metaphor is of a picture puzzle with some of the pieces missing. *Maybe* is more introspective than the earlier memoirs, revealing more about Hellman than the small cast of principal characters: acquaintance Sarah Cameron; Sarah's husband, Carter Cameron; their son, Som; and Sarah's friend Ferry. They are shallow people who may be shrouding malice in pleasantries and evil in sociability. As they appear, disappear, and reappear, the tone is qualified and questioning, frequently repeating the title word and the word "time."

Sarah is a casual acquaintance, "a kind of interesting drop-in," who persists in dropping into the account like a disturbing character in a dream. The book opens with Sarah: "It was always with Sarah this way and that way all over the place, or maybe I never saw enough to understand. At a few points I know what happened, but there's a good deal I don't, because of time or because I didn't much care."

Sarah is flighty, hates to think, and cares nothing about time—characteristics directly opposed to Hellman's. As Sarah's husband explains: "It's not a question of life or people with Sarah. She has no interest in tomorrow because she has no interest in yesterday. It comes down to hours."

In this scattered recollection, Sarah figures in two memorable episodes. When young, both have an affair with a malicious young man named Alex, who, after intercourse tells Hellman that she has "an interesting but strange odor." Thereafter, Hellman "couldn't go to bed with anybody with pleasure, without nerves and fear" (20). After "years of worry," Sarah frees Hellman from her gynephobia by confiding that Alex had told her the same thing (18).

Death is the single unspoken subject of *Maybe*. Hellman was seventy-five when *Maybe* was published. She was to live four more years, nearly blind and with the increasing pain of emphysema and heart trouble. She refers to her failing eyesight and her shortness of breath, but death is mentioned only in relation to others. An interlude in New Orleans concerns her aunts Hannah and Jenny: "now neither beloved woman would be here for me much longer, and I knew already the forever-deprivation of that" (76). When Hellman visits her Aunt Hannah in the hospital, the doctor tells her, "there probably wasn't long to go" (83). Contrasted to this factual and at-times humorous account is the dreamlike sequence about Lady Ottoline Morrell.

Lost in a forest in France, Hellman comes upon a chateau where a man and a woman are sitting upon a terrace but do not speak to her. Third in the trio is Sarah, who drives Hellman back to her hotel in an ancient, hearselike, open Rolls Royce and announces that Lady Ottoline Morrell, the woman on the terrace, expects her for dinner and will send the car around nine. The car never arrives. Hellman learns that Lady Ottoline had died ten years earlier.

Another link between Sarah and death is similarly bizarre. A New Year's invitation from Ferry, a malicious gossip, closes with the news that Sarah is dead. Many years later, Hellman learns that Sarah faked her death in Italy so that her son could benefit from her large insurance policy.

The final section of *Maybe* centers upon Hellman's relationship with Sarah's former husband, Carter Cameron. Over seven or eight years they are together "maybe twenty or thirty times," in New York or in San Francisco, where he lives, or in the Leeward Islands, where they sail. "The times we slept together were calm without passion, but it was, and is, one of the happy arrangements of my life" (84).

Her last meeting with Cameron is strange and awkward. In a restaurant, her eyesight fails for the first time and she can see nothing beyond ten feet. Then Cameron, in a tone that is "terrible" and "false," invites her to go sailing. She can only stare at him, and he admits, "You caught me, yes?" "What did you say it for?" she asks. "I've never done anything to you." "But you might," he replies, "you just might." The atmosphere has darkened; the mood is reflected in Hellman's inability to "see" (95).

Darkness encompasses the final incident at Martha's Vineyard, when Hellman decides to go for a swim one evening, is unable to see the shore, but reaches it by following the sound of waves hitting a breakwater. Finding her way home with great difficulty, she lies down and sleeps briefly. "When I woke up the world seemed gone. I was in the kind of temper that has no name because it is not temper but was some monumental despair that makes crazy people kill cats or stifle crying babies." She sends a telegram to Carter Cameron at his telephone number: "THERE ARE MISSING PIECES EVERYPLACE AND EVERYWHERE AND THEY ARE NOT MY BUSINESS UNLESS THEY TOUCH ME. BUT WHEN THEY TOUCH ME, I DO NOT WISH THEM TO BE BLACK. MY INSTINCT REPEAT INSTINCT REPEAT INSTINCT REPEAT INSTINCT IS THAT YOURS ARE BLACK. LILLIAN." Western Union phones her two days later to say there is no Mr. Cameron at the telephone number on the telegram. She phones. A man answers and says he has never heard of Mr. Cameron. "I hung up," the book concludes (101–2).

Carter Cameron, like the others, seems to have vanished or maybe changed his name. Sarah, whose real name was Melaniess, changes to a new persona, Signora Pinelli, who in Rome claims not to know Hellman. When Sarah "dies," the corpse of an Italian woman is purchased and buried under the name of Sarah Cameron Petraccini, and Sarah then assumes Ferry's name (98). Sarah's son is named Isaac, yet called Som for "son of many," because she "slept around," but he looks, to Carter's regret, "exactly like" Carter (88).

Maybe raises questions to which the only reply might be the single word of the title. Does its subtitle, "a story," mean it is a parable or allegory, with additional, more significant, meanings beyond the literal narrative? Might the Camerons embody a vaguely sensed, only to be guessed at, threat that might destroy one who cannot recognize evil and mistakes it for good? Som describes himself as "dangerous," the same word his father uses for him. When his distorted looks remind Hellman of the makeup job that transformed her friend Boris Karloff into Frankenstein, is this a warning? Both Som and his mother take dope. Does it change them into other persons or personalities? Do the black pieces, fitted together, reveal a picture of Death?

Is Sarah an alter ego of Hellman's? As young women, both sleep with Alex and later in life with Carter. Both see life as a picture puzzle. When Sarah frees Hellman from the obsession that prevented her from enjoying sex, is Hellman freed by Sarah's story or by her own realization that Alex made the charge out of malice? (She sees him fifteen years later and recognizes the malice she did not see before.)

Although they are opposites in character, Sarah possesses physical attributes that Hellman has always, in vain, longed for. Sarah is beautiful, as Hellman regretted she was not. The scene of twenty-five-year-old Sarah dancing in a Harlem nightclub epitomizes the jazz age—her gown slips off her shoulders to reveal her breasts, and her "fair hair" is piled high. (Hellman lamented having "stringy" hair.) Perhaps of most significance in this story or parable: does Sarah achieve what the aging Hellman knows to be impossible? Does Sarah defeat Death?

In her recollections Hellman is almost deliberately indefinite as to time. (Perhaps this was her way of responding to critics who tried to pinpoint in time incidents in the memoirs.) Sometimes the spareness, the significance of the unsaid, the silences, the abrupt shifts are reminiscent of Samuel Beckett, whose dramas Hellman admired. The style of *Maybe* marks a new direction for Hellman, who welcomed the idea: "There are a thousand ways to write, and each is as good as the other if it fits you, if you are any good. If you can break into a new pattern along the way, and it opens things up, and allows you more freedom, that's something."[1]

Unlike the previous memoirs, with imagery based upon everyday life, here symbols are drawn from nature: a lake, a forest, the ocean, daylight, and night. The black of the Rolls Royce, of the night swim, and of the missing pieces evokes the black of a grave.

There are two internal monologues. The first is a short, poetic rumination on the passage of time, beginning "The piles and bundles and ribbons and rags turn into years, and then the years are gone." One sentence encapsulates a lifetime during which carefully saved memories—substantial piles and bundles—disintegrate into flimsy rags and strips as years pass, and then, like the years, "are gone." The metaphor in which the substantial turns fragile and then vanishes is repeated: the "solid wall of convictions now seems on bad nights, or in sickness, or just weakness, no longer made of much that can be leaned against." Recollection requires one to "dig" and "sometimes you are frightened that near an edge is nothing" (42). Even while drawing nearer that edge, Hellman continues to dig.

The second monologue deals with the nature of truth: "In the three memoir books I wrote, I tried very hard for the truth. I did try, but here I don't know much of what really happened and never tried to find out. In addition to the ordinary deceptions that you and others make in your life, time itself makes time fuzzy and meshes truth with half truth." The metaphor is that of a picture puzzle: "It's as if I have fitted parts of a picture puzzle and then a child overturned it and threw out some pieces" (51–52).

The tone of *Maybe* differs substantially from that of the earlier memoirs. In the first two, Hellman is enthusiastic about her subjects, people who are worth knowing. In *Scoundrel Time* the villains are presented with irony and humor. In *Maybe,* with Hammett on the periphery in the earlier events and dead in the later ones, one might hope never to meet any of the other characters. Hellman's oblique, tangential account implies that these people not only are distasteful, but are to be feared. Beneath their pleasant exteriors may lurk what cannot be seen: inexpressible, unfathomable danger. They become more dangerous as the narrative progresses and the atmosphere darkens.

Yet Hellman survives. Eyesight failing, she makes her way back in the dark in the final episode, which ends with her identifying the "missing pieces" as "black," and, instinctively, breaking off her relationship with Cameron. The book ends as it began. Now, as Sarah did in the opening episode, Cameron has disappeared. Maybe.

Chapter 1: Career

1. John Hersey, "Lillian Hellman," in *Critical Essays on Lillian Hellman*, ed. Mark W. Estrin (Boston: G. K. Hall, 1989), 249.

2. Anne Hollander and John Phillips, "Lillian Hellman," in *Writers at Work: The Paris Review Interviews*, 3d ser., ed. George Plimpton (New York: Viking, 1967), 128.

3. Christine Doudna, "A Still Unfinished Woman," *Rolling Stone*, 24 February 1977, 57.

4. William Roughead, "Closed Doors; or, The Great Drumsheugh Case," in *Bad Companions* (Edinburgh: W. Green & Son, 1930), 111–46. Lillian Faderman interprets the trial in *Scotch Verdict* (New York: Quill, 1983).

5. Thomas Meehan, "An Interview with Lillian Hellman," in *The Modern Theatre*, ed. Robert W. Corrigan (New York: Macmillan, 1964), 1112.

6. "Day in Spain," *New Republic* 94 (13 April 1938): 297–98. "The Little War," in *This Is My Best*, ed. Whitney Burnett (New York: Dial, 1942), 989–96.

7. Meehan, "An Interview," 1109.

8. Lucius Beebe, "An Adult's Hour Is Miss Hellman's Next Effort" (1936), in *Conversations with Lillian Hellman*, ed. Jackson R. Bryer (Jackson: University Press of Mississippi), 5.

9. Richard Poirier, "Introduction," in *Three* (Boston: Little, Brown, 1979), xvi.

10. Stephanie dePue, "Lillian Hellman: She Never Turns Down an Adventure" (1975), in *Conversations with Lillian Hellman*, ed. Jackson R. Bryer (Jackson: University Press of Mississippi, 1986), 188.

11. Brooks Atkinson, *Broadway* (New York: Macmillan, 1970), 299.

12. Robert P. Newman, *The Cold War Romance of Lillian Hellman and John Melby* (Chapel Hill: University of North Carolina Press, 1989), 32.

13. Bernard F. Dick, *Hellman in Hollywood* (Rutherford, N.J. : Fairleigh Dickinson, 1982), 101.

14. Newman, *Cold War Romance,* 34.

15. Marilyn Berger, "Profile: Lillian Hellman" (1979), Public Broadcasting System five-part series, in *Conversations with Lillian Hellman,* ed. Jackson R. Bryer (Jackson: University Press of Mississippi, 1986), 257.

16. Lillian Hellman, "Introduction," in *The Selected Letters of Anton Chekhov* (New York: Farrar, Straus, 1955), xiii, xiv, xix, xxv.

17. Alice Griffin, "Books—Of a Different Feather: Lillian Hellman's *The Lark,*" *Theatre Arts Magazine* 40 (May 1956), 8–10.

18. Carl Rollyson, *Lillian Hellman* (New York: St. Martin's, 1988), 353.

19. Gerald Weales, *American Drama Since World War II* (New York: Harcourt, Brace, 1962), 152–53.

20. Atkinson, *Broadway,* 446.

21. Jacob H. Adler, "The Rose and the Fox: Notes on the Southern Drama," in *South: Modern Southern Literature in Its Cultural Setting,* ed. Louis D. Rubin Jr. and Robert D. Jacobs (Garden City, N.Y.: Doubleday, 1961), 373–74.

22. Charlotte Goodman, "The Fox's Cubs: Lillian Hellman, Arthur Miller, and Tennessee Williams," in *Modern American Drama: The Female Canon,* ed. June Schlueter (Rutherford, N.J.: Fairleigh Dickinson, 1990), 137, 141. It has been pointed out that *The Children's Hour* may have influenced Arthur Miller's *The Crucible.*

23. Poirier, "Introduction," xvii, xviii–xix, xv.

24. Mark W. Estrin, "Introduction," *Critical Essays on Lillian Hellman,* ed. Mark W. Estrin (Boston: G. K. Hall, 1989), 20.

25. Bill Moyers, "Lillian Hellman," in *Conversations with Lillian Hellman,* ed. Jackson R. Bryer (Jackson: University Press of Mississippi, 1986), 149; Christine Doudna, "A Still Unfinished Woman," 56.

26. Margaret Case Harriman, "Miss Lily of New Orleans: Lillian Hellman," in *Take Them up Tenderly* (New York: Knopf, 1944), 95.

27. George Jean Nathan, "The Status of the Female Playwrights," in *The Entertainment of a Nation* (Rutherford, N.J.: Fairleigh Dickinson, 1971), 34–37.

28. Marcus K. Billson and Sidonie A. Smith, "Lillian Hellman and the Strategy of the 'Other,'" in *Women's Autobiography: Essays in Criticism,* ed. Estelle C. Jelinek (Bloomington: Indiana University Press, 1980), 163. See also Susanne Mayer, *Die Sehnsucht nach den Anderen* (Frankfurt: Peter Lang, 1986).

29. Estrin, "Introduction," 17.

30. Martha Gellhorn, "On Apocryphism," *Paris Review* (spring 1981), in *Critical Essays on Lillian Hellman,* ed. Mark W. Estrin (Boston: G. K. Hall, 1989), 175–90.

31. Rollyson, *Lillian Hellman,* 396–406.

32. Manfred Triesch, *The Lillian Hellman Collection at the University of Texas* (Austin: University of Texas Press, 1966), 24–25, 105–7.

33. Hollander and Phillips, "Lillian Hellman," 131.

34. Lyle Leverich, *Tom* (New York: Crown, 1995), 328. George Jean Nathan's advice to the "Stagestruck" included: "If you have a Southern accent, get rid of it"; Nathan, *Entertainment,* 145.

35. Jacob H. Adler, *Lillian Hellman,* Southern Writers Series 4 (Austin, Tex.: Steck-Vaughn, 1969), 4.

36. Harold Clurman, "Lillian Hellman," in *Lies Like Truth* (New York: Macmillan, 1958), 47.

37. John Gassner, "Lillian Hellman: *The Autumn Garden,*" in *Theatre at the Crossroads* (New York: Holt, Rinehart, 1960), 134.

38. Triesch, *Collection,* 74.

39. Estrin, *Lillian Hellman,* 3.

40. Robert W. Corrigan, ed., *The Modern Theatre* (New York: Macmillan, 1964), 1074.

41. Katherine Lederer, *Lillian Hellman* (Boston: Twayne, 1979), 35.

42. Gassner, *Theatre,* 138.

43. Fred Gardner, "An Interview with Lillian Hellman" (1968), in *Conversations with Lillian Hellman,* ed. Jackson R. Bryer (Jackson: University Press of Mississippi, 1986), 116.

44. Ellen Moers, *Literary Women* (London: W. H. Allen, 1977), 77.

45. Poirier, "Introduction," ix–x.

46. Patricia M. Spacks, *The Female Imagination* (New York: Knopf, 1975), 298–99.

47. Sylvie Drake, "Lillian Hellman as Herself" (1981), in *Conversations with Lillian Hellman,* ed. Jackson R. Bryer (Jackson: University Press of Mississippi, 1986), 289.

48. Meehan, "An Interview," 1109.

49. Hellman, "Introduction," *Selected Letters,* xxiv–xxv.

50. Ibid., ix.

51. Rollyson, *Hellman,* 549.

52. Peter Feibleman, *Lilly* (New York: William Morrow, 1988), 344, 349.

Chapter 2: *The Children's Hour*

1. Harry Gilroy, "The Bigger the Lie," in *The Children's Hour: Acting Edition* (New York: Dramatists Play Service, 1953), 3.

2. Ibid.

3. Margaret Case Harriman, "Miss Lily of New Orleans: Lillian Hellman," in *Take Them up Tenderly* (New York: Knopf, 1944), 102.

4. Philip M. Armato, "'Good and Evil' in Lillian Hellman's *The Children's Hour,* in *Critical Essays on Lillian Hellman,* ed. Mark W. Estrin (Boston: G. K. Hall, 1989), 73–78.

5. Fred Gardner, "An Interview with Lillian Hellman" (1968), in *Conversations with Lillian Hellman,* ed. Jackson R. Bryer (Jackson: University Press of Mississippi, 1986), 110.

6. Judith Olauson, *The American Woman Playwright: A View of Criticism and Characterization* (Troy, N.Y.: Whitston, 1981), 34.

7. Jacob Adler, "The Dramaturgy of Blackmail in the Ibsenite Hellman," in *Critical Essays on Lillian Hellman,* ed. Mark W. Estrin (Boston: G. K. Hall, 1989), 34.

8. Mary Lynn Broe, "Bohemia Bumps into Calvin: The Deception of Passivity in Lillian Hellman's Drama," in *Critical Essays on Lillian Hellman,* ed. Mark W. Estrin (Boston: G. K. Hall, 1989), 82.

9. Carl Rollyson, *Lillian Hellman: Her Legend and Her Legacy* (New York: St. Martin's, 1988), 66.

10. Manfred Triesch, *The Lillian Hellman Collection at the University of Texas* (Austin: University of Texas Press, 1966), 104.

11. Gardner, "Interview," 111.

12. Mark W. Estrin, "Introduction," in *Critical Essays on Lillian Hellman,* ed. Mark W. Estrin (Boston: G. K. Hall, 1989), 2.

Chapter 3: *Another Part of the Forest* and *The Little Foxes*

1. Robert B. Heilman, *The Iceman, the Arsonist, and the Troubled Agent* (Seattle: University of Washington Press, 1973), 301–2.

2. Manfred Triesch, *The Lillian Hellman Collection at the University of Texas* (Austin: University of Texas Press, 1966), 24–25.

3. Jacob H. Adler, "The Rose and the Fox," in *South: Modern Southern Literature in Its Cultural Setting,* ed. Louis D. Rubin Jr. and Robert D. Jacobs (Garden City, N.Y.: Doubleday, 1961), 370.

4. Brooks Atkinson, *Broadway* (New York: Macmillan, 1970), 300, and *The New York Times,* 21 November 1946.

5. Lillian Hellman, "Introduction," *The Selected Letters of Anton Chekhov* (New York: Farrar, Straus, 1955), xxiii–iv.

6. Lucius Beebe, "Miss Hellman Talks of Her Latest Play, *The Little Foxes,* " in *Conversations with Lillian Hellman,* ed. Jackson R. Bryer (Jackson: University Press of Mississippi, 1986), 7–8.

7. Triesch, *Collection,* 106.

8. Ibid., 105.

9. In Hellman's first three versions, she notes in *Pentimento,* 172, "because it had been true in life, Horace Giddens had syphilis."

10. Hellman uses the words of her great-uncle Jake, the inspiration for Ben, when as a young woman she told Jake that she had hocked his graduation present, a ring, to buy books. *Unfinished Woman,* 4–5.

11. Anne Hollander and John Phillips, "The Art of the Theater: Lillian Hellman, an Interview," in *Writers at Work: The Paris Review Interviews,* 3d ser., ed. George Plimpton (New York: Viking, 1967), 121.

12. Charlotte Goodman, "The Fox's Cubs: Lillian Hellman, Arthur Miller, and Tennessee Williams," in *Modern American Drama: The Female Canon,* ed. June Schlueter (Rutherford, N.J.: Fairleigh Dickinson, 1990), 137.

13. Lyle Leverich, *Tom* (New York: Crown, 1995), 328.

Chapter 4: *Watch on the Rhine*

1. Mark W. Estrin, "Introduction," in *Critical Essays on Lillian Hellman,* ed. Mark W. Estrin (Boston: G. K. Hall, 1980), 7.

2. The *New York Post,* 24 October 1941.

3. *The New Yorker* 17 (12 April 1941), 32.

4. Margaret Case Harriman, "Miss Lily of New Orleans: Lillian Hellman," in *Take Them up Tenderly* (New York: Knopf, 1944), 104.

5. Timothy J. Wiles, "Lillian Hellman's American Political Theater: The Thirties and Beyond," in *Critical Essays on Lillian Hellman,* ed. Mark W. Estrin (Boston: G. K. Hall, 1980), 93.

6. Vivian M. Patraka, "Lillian Hellman's *Watch on the Rhine:* Realism, Gender and Historical Crisis," *Modern Drama* 32, no. 1 (March 1989): 129.

7. Rollyson, *Lillian Hellman,* 195.

8. Patraka, "Lillian Hellman's *Watch on the Rhine,*" 131.

Chapter 5: *The Autumn Garden*

1. Mark W. Estrin, "Introduction," in *Critical Essays on Lillian Hellman,* ed. Mark W. Estrin (Boston: G. K. Hall, 1980), 13.

2. Marvin Felheim, "*The Autumn Garden*: Mechanics and Dialectics," in *Critical Essays on Lillian Hellman,* ed. Mark W. Estrin (Boston: G. K. Hall, 1980), 52.

3. Harold Clurman, *"The Autumn Garden,"* in *On Directing* (New York: Macmillan, 1972), 205.

4. Jacob Adler, "The Dramaturgy of Blackmail in the Ibsenite Hellman," in *Critical Essays on Lillian Hellman,* ed. Mark W. Estrin (Boston: G. K. Hall, 1980), 36, 38.

5. Perhaps Hellman is remembering the preface she wrote for her first collection of plays in 1942: "there is much in all the plays that is wrong," yet "this much has been right: I tried. I did the best I could at the time . . . . Within the limitations of my own mind and nature, my own understanding, my own knowledge, it was the best I could do with what I had."

6. Clurman, *"The Autumn Garden,"* 203.

7. Carole Klein and Richard Gotti, *Overcoming Regret* (New York: Bantam, 1992), 68.

8. Clurman, *"The Autumn Garden,"* 198.

9. Ibid., 199.

10. Gerald Weales, *American Drama Since World War II* (New York: Harcourt, Brace, 1962), 91.

11. Felheim, *"Autumn Garden,"* 53.

Chapter 6: *Toys in the Attic*

1. Katherine Lederer, *Lillian Hellman* (Boston: Twayne, 1979), 94.

2. Lorena Ross Holmin, *The Dramatic Works of Lillian Hellman* (Stockholm: Rotobeckman, 1973), 149.

3. Tom Scanlon, *Family, Drama, and American Dreams* (Westport, Conn.: Greenwood, 1978), 184.

4. Jacob H. Adler, "Miss Hellman's Two Sisters," *Educational Theatre Journal* 15 (May 1963): 113.

5. Charles Child Walcutt, *Man's Changing Masks: Modes of Characterization in Fiction* (Minneapolis: University of Minnesota Press, 1966), 30–31.

6. Alan S. Downer, *Recent American Drama* (Minneapolis: University of Minnesota Press, 1961), 42.

7. Lederer, *Hellman,* 102.

8. Walcutt, *Masks,* 31.

9. Downer, *American Drama,* 41.

Chapter 7: *An Unfinished Woman* and *Pentimento*

1. Pamela S. Bromberg, "Establishing the Woman and Constructing a Narrative in Lillian Hellman's Memoirs," in *Critical*

Essays on Lillian Hellman, ed. Mark W. Estrin (Boston: G. K. Hall, 1989), 122.

2. Timothy Dow Adams, "'Lies Like Truth': Lillian Hellman's Autobiographies," in *Critical Essays on Lillian Hellman,* ed. Mark W. Estrin (Boston: G. K. Hall, 1989), 198.

3. Bromberg, "Memoirs," 117.

4. "The Little War," in *This Is My Best,* ed. Whit Burnett (New York: Dial Press, 1942), 989–96. In this anthology of pieces self-chosen by "America's 93 greatest living authors," Hellman writes in her preface to "these pieces from a diary written on a long trip to Europe in 1937 . . . about Spain during the Civil War," that "I don't know whether they are my favorites. I don't even know whether I have favorite pieces of writing. I do know that I hope these people are alive, that they will live to see a better day."

5. Bromberg, "Memoirs," 115–16.

6. Ibid., 116.

7. William C. Spengemann, *The Forms of Autobiography* (New Haven: Yale University Press, 1980), xvi.

8. James Olney, *Metaphors of Self: The Meaning of Autobiography* (Princeton: Princeton University Press, 1972), x.

9. Mary G. Mason, "The Other Voice: Autobiographies of Women Writers," in *Autobiography: Essays Theoretical and Critical,* ed. James Olney (Princeton: Princeton University Press, 1980), 231–32.

10. Bromberg, "Memoirs," 117.

11. Rex Reed, "Lillian Hellman" (1975), in *Conversations with Lillian Hellman,* ed. Jackson R. Bryer (Jackson: University Press of Mississippi, 1986), 181.

12. Carl Rollyson, *Lillian Hellman: Her Legend and Her Legacy* (New York: St. Martin's, 1988), 512–28.

13. Ibid., 518–23.

14. Martha Gellhorn, "Close Encounters of the Apocryphal Kind," in *Critical Essays on Lillian Hellman,* ed. Mark W. Estrin (Boston: G. K. Hall, 1989), 175–90.

15. Rollyson, *Lillian Hellman,* 515–16.

16. Ibid., 528.

17. Theodore Miller, *Disorders of Personality* (New York: John Wiley, 1996), 359, 363–69.

18. Anne Hollander and John Phillips, "The Art of the Theater: Lillian Hellman, an Interview," in *Writers at Work,* 3d ser., ed. George Plimpton (New York: Viking, 1967), 131.

Chapter 8: *Scoundrel Time*

1. Diane Johnson, *Dashiell Hammett: A Life* (New York: Random House, 1983), 3–12, 238–49.

2. Katherine Lederer, *Lillian Hellman* (Boston: Twayne, 1979), 10, 27.

3. House Un-American Activities Committee, *Communist Infiltration of the Hollywood Motion-Picture Industry: Hearings before the Committee on Un-American Activities, House of Representatives,* 82d Cong., 2d sess., pt. 8, 19–21 May 1952. Washington, D.C.: U.S. Government Printing Office, 3541–49.

4. Arthur Miller, "Why I Wrote *The Crucible,*" *The New Yorker* 72 no. 32 (21, 28 October 1996): 159.

5. Anne Hollander and John Phillips, "The Art of the Theater: Lillian Hellman, an Interview," in *Writers at Work,* 3d ser., ed. George Plimpton (New York: Viking, 1967), 133.

6. Mark W. Estrin, *Lillian Hellman: Plays, Films, Memoirs* (Boston: G. K. Hall, 1980), 305–43.

7. William Phillips, "What Happened in the Fifties," *Partisan*

Review 43 (fall 1976): 337–40; Nathan Glazer, "An Answer to Lillian Hellman," *Commentary* 61 (19 June 1976): 36–39.

8. William F. Buckley Jr., "Who Is the Ugliest of Them All?" *National Review* 29 (21 January 1977): 101–6.

9. Timothy Dow Adams, "Lies Like Truth': Lillian Hellman's Autobiographies," in *Critical Essays on Lillian Hellman,* ed. Mark W. Estrin (Boston: G. K. Hall, 1989), 198.

10. Robert Sherrill, "Wisdom and Its Price," *The Nation* 222 (19 June 1976): 757–58.

Chapter 9: *Maybe*

1. Anne Hollander and John Phillips, "The Art of the Theater: Lillian Hellman, an Interview" in *Writers at Work,* 3d ser., ed. George Plimpton (New York: Viking, 1967), 123.

BIBLIOGRAPHY

Primary Works

Complete Collection

The Collected Plays. Boston: Little, Brown, 1972. London: Macmillan, 1974. Twelve plays with Hellman's "revisions and emendations."

Plays

The Children's Hour. New York: Alfred Knopf, 1934. London: Hamish Hamilton, 1937. Acting edition, New York: Dramatists Play Service, 1953.

Days to Come. New York, London: Alfred Knopf, 1936.

The Little Foxes. New York: Random House, 1939. London: Hamish Hamilton, 1939. Acting edition, New York: Dramatists Play Service, 1942.

Watch on the Rhine. New York: Random House, 1941. London: English Theatre Guild, 1941. Acting edition, New York: Dramatists Play Service, 1944.

Four Plays. (The Children's Hour, Days to Come, The Little Foxes, Watch on the Rhine) New York: Random House Modern Library, 1942.

The Searching Wind. New York: Viking, 1944.

Another Part of the Forest. New York: Viking, 1947. Acting edition, New York: Dramatists Play Service, 1948.

Montserrat. New York: Dramatists Play Service, 1950.

The Autumn Garden. Boston: Little, Brown, 1951. Acting edition, New York: Dramatists Play Service, 1952.

The Lark. New York: Random House, 1956. Acting edition, New York: Dramatists Play Service, 1957.

Candide, A Comic Operetta Based on Voltaire's Satire. Book by Lillian Hellman, score by Leonard Bernstein, lyrics by Richard Wilbur. New York: Random House, 1957.

Toys in the Attic. New York: Random House, 1960. Acting edition, New York: Dramatists Play Service, 1978.

Six Plays. (The Children's Hour, Days to Come, the Little Foxes, Watch on the Rhine, Another Part of the Forest, The Autumn Garden) New York: Modern Library, 1960.

My Mother, My Father and Me. New York: Random House, 1963. Acting edition, New York: Dramatists Play Service, 1964.

Memoirs

An Unfinished Woman: A Memoir. Boston: Little, Brown, 1969. London: Macmillan, 1969.

Pentimento: A Book of Portraits. Boston: Little, Brown, 1973. London: Macmillan, 1974.

Scoundrel Time. Introduction by Garry Wills. Boston: Little, Brown, 1976. Introduction by James Cameron (for British readers). Commentary by Garry Wills. London: Macmillan, 1976.

Three. (An Unfinished Woman, Pentimento, Scoundrel Time) With new commentaries by the author. Introduction by Richard Poirier. Boston: Little, Brown, 1979. London: Macmillan, 1979.

Maybe: A Story. Boston: Little, Brown, 1980. London: Macmillan, 1980.

Eating Together: Recollections and Recipes . With Peter Feibleman. Boston: Little, Brown, 1984. London: Chatto and Windus, 1989.

Books Edited

The Selected Letters of Anton Chekhov. Edited and with an introduc-
tion by Lillian Hellman. New York: Farrar, Straus, 1955. London:
Hamish Hamilton, 1955.
*The Big Knockover: Selected Short Stories and Short Novels of
Dashiell Hammett.* Edited and with an introduction by Lillian Hell-
man. New York: Random House, 1966. London: Cassell, 1966.

Screenplays

The Dark Angel. Adapted, with Mordaunt Sharp, from the play by
Guy Bolton, 1935.
These Three. First screen adaptation of *The Children's Hour,* 1936.
Dead End. Adapted from the play by Sidney Kingsley, 1937.
The Little Foxes. With additional dialogue by Dorothy Parker, Arthur
Kober, and Alan Campbell, 1941.
The North Star. New York: Viking, 1943.
Watch on the Rhine. Hellman wrote additional scenes and dialogue for
the screenplay by Dashiell Hammett, 1943.
The Searching Wind, 1946.
The Chase. Based on a novel and a play by Horton Foote, 1966.

Selected Miscellaneous Writings

"I Call Her Mama Now." *American Spectator* 1 (September 1933): 2.
"Perberty in Los Angeles." *American Spectator* 2 (January 1934): 4.
"Day in Spain." *New Republic* 94 (13 April 1938): 297–98.
"Back of Those Foxes." *New York Times,* 26 February 1939, sec. 9,
1–2.

"The Little War." In *This Is My Best,* edited by Whitney Burnett, 989–96. New York: Dial, 1942.

"I Meet the Front-Line Russians." *Collier's* 115 (31 March 1945): 11, 68, 71.

"Author Jabs the Critics." *New York Times,* 15 December 1946, sec. 2, 3–4.

"The Judas Goats." *Screen Writer* 3 (December 1947): 7.

"Sophronia's Grandson Goes to Washington." *Ladies Home Journal* 80 (December 1963): 78–80, 82.

"For Truth, Justice, and the American Way." Commencement address, Barnard College, *New York Times,* 4 June 1975, 39.

"Plain Speaking with Mrs. [Rosalynn] Carter." *Rolling Stone* 226 (18 November 1976): 43–45.

Adaptations by Others of Hellman's Works

Another Part of the Forest. Screenplay by Vladimir Pozner, 1948.

Regina. Opera by Marc Blitzstein based on *The Little Foxes,* 1949. New York: Chappel, 1954.

The Children's Hour. Screenplay by John Michael Hayes. Second screen version, 1962.

Toys in the Attic. Screenplay by James Poe, 1963.

Julia. Screenplay by Alvin Sargent, based on the "Julia" chapter in *Pentimento,* 1977.

Secondary Works

Bibliography

Bills, Steven H. *Lillian Hellman: An Annotated Bibliography.* New York: Garland, 1979.

BIBLIOGRAPHY

Estrin, Mark W. *Lillian Hellman: Plays, Films, Memoirs.* Boston: G. K. Hall, 1980. Comprehensive, accurate, dependable evaluations, well-chosen quotes.

Riordan, Mary. *Lillian Hellman: A Bibliography, 1926–1978.* Metuchen, N.J.: Scarecrow, 1980.

Critical Studies: Books

Adler, Jacob H. *Lillian Hellman.* Southern Writers Series 4. Austin, Tex.: Steck-Vaughn, 1969. Perceptive analysis and original insights.

Bryer, Jackson R., ed. *Conversations with Lillian Hellman.* Jackson: University Press of Mississippi, 1986. Excellent selection of interviews, including PBS Berger.

Dick, Bernard F. *Hellman in Hollywood.* Rutherford, N.J.: Fairleigh Dickinson, 1982. Good coverage of Hellman's screenplays and others' film adaptations of her works.

Downer, Alan S. *Recent American Drama.* Minneapolis: University of Minnesota Press, 1961. Useful analyses of Hellman plays and those of her contemporaries.

Estrin, Mark W., ed. *Critical Essays on Lillian Hellman.* Boston: G. K. Hall, 1989. Excellent long introduction by editor Estrin; good essays on Hellman's plays, persona, and memoirs.

Falk, Doris V. *Lillian Hellman.* New York: Ungar, 1978. Simplistic division of characters into "despoilers" and "bystanders."

Feibleman, Peter. *Lilly: Reminiscences of Lillian Hellman.* New York: William Morrow, 1988. London: Chatto and Windus, 1989. Recollections by friend and lover.

Heilman, Robert B. *The Iceman, the Arsonist, and the Troubled Agent: Tragedy and Melodrama on the Modern Stage.* Seattle: University of Washington Press, 1973. *The Little Foxes* as melodrama.

BIBLIOGRAPHY

Holmin, Lorena Ross. *The Dramatic Works of Lillian Hellman.* Stockholm: Rotobeckman, 1973.

Klein, Carole, and Richard Gotti. *Overcoming Regret.* New York: Bantam, 1992. Useful for interpreting *The Autumn Garden.*

Johnson, Diane. *Dashiell Hammett: A Life.* New York: Random House, 1983. Lively and readable account.

Lacan, Jacques. *Escrits* (1960). Translated by Alan Sheridan. London: Tavistock, 1977. Standard reference for studies of autobiography.

Layman, Richard. *Shadow Man: The Life of Dashiell Hammett.* New York: Harcourt, Brace, 1981. Dependable, factual account.

Lederer, Katherine. *Lillian Hellman.* Boston: Twayne, 1979. Good overall analyses; interesting and helpful insights.

Leverich, Lyle. *Tom: The Unknown Tennessee Williams.* New York: Crown, 1995. Confirms Hellman influence on Williams.

Mayer, Susanne. *Die Sehnsucht nach den Anderen.* Frankfurt: Lang, 1986. Importance of memoirs about others, like *Pentimento,* in revealing the writer.

Miller, Theodore, with Roger D. Davis. *Disorders of Personality.* New York: John Wiley, 1996. Diagnosis of "histrionic" personality disorder fits Arthur A. W. Cowan to a T.

Moers, Ellen. *Literary Women.* Garden City, N.Y.: Doubleday, 1976. London: W. H. Allen, 1977. Required reading.

Moody, Richard. *Lillian Hellman: Playwright.* New York: Pegasus, 1972. Neither analytical nor insightful, but good on details of original productions.

Nathan, George Jean. *The Entertainment of a Nation.* 1942. Rutherford, N.J.: Fairleigh Dickinson, 1971. An erstwhile "dean" of drama critics considers women dramatists inferior to men; warns against using southern speech on stage.

Newman, Robert P. *The Cold War Romance of Lillian Hellman and*

BIBLIOGRAPHY

John Melby. Chapel Hill: University of North Carolina Press, 1989.

Olauson, Judith. *The American Woman Playwright: A View of Criticism and Characterization.* Troy, N.Y.: Whitston, 1981.

Olney, James. *Metaphors of Self: The Meaning of Autobiography.* Princeton: Princeton University Press, 1972. Impressive exploration of theories and language in autobiographies.

Rollyson, Carl. *Lillian Hellman: Her Legend and Her Legacy.* New York: St. Martin's, 1988. Detailed and objective, best biography to date.

Scanlon, Tom. *Family, Drama, and American Dreams.* Westport, Conn.: Greenwood, 1978. Considers Hellman's family-centered dramas.

Spacks, Patricia Meyer. *The Female Imagination.* New York: Knopf, 1975. London: George Aken, 1976. Early feminist work analyzes Hellman's persona.

Spengemann, William C. *The Forms of Autobiography: Episodes in the History of a Literary Genre.* New Haven: Yale University Press, 1980. Defines characteristics of historical, philosophical, and poetic autobiography applicable to Hellman's memoirs. Useful bibliographical essay.

Triesch, Manfred. *The Lillian Hellman Collection at the University of Texas.* Austin: University of Texas Press, 1966. Hellman's first drafts, notes, and notebooks.

Walcutt, Charles Child. *Man's Changing Masks: Modes of Characterization in Fiction.* Minneapolis: University of Minnesota Press, 1966.

Weales, Gerald. *American Drama Since World War II.* New York: Harcourt, Brace, 1962. Perceptive, detailed analyses of Hellman's dramas and book for *Candide.*

Wright, William. *Lillian Hellman: The Image, The Woman.* New York: Simon & Schuster, 1986. From interviews with Hellman detractors.

BIBLIOGRAPHY

Critical Studies: Articles and Chapters in Books

Adams, Timothy Dow. "'Lies Like Truth': Lillian Hellman's Autobiographies." In *Critical Essays on Lillian Hellman,* edited by Mark W. Estrin, 194–216. Boston: G. K. Hall, 1989.

Adler, Jacob H. "Miss Hellman's Two Sisters." *Educational Theatre Journal* 15 (May 1963): 112–17. Relates *Toys in the Attic* to Chekhov.

———. "The Rose and the Fox: Notes on the Southern Drama." In *South: Modern Southern Literature in Its Cultural Setting,* edited by Louis D. Rubin Jr. and Robert D. Jacobs, 349–75. Garden City, N.Y.: Doubleday, 1961.

Armato, Philip M. "'Good and Evil' in Lillian Hellman's *The Children's Hour.*" In *Critical Essays on Lillian Hellman,* edited by Mark W. Estrin, 73–78. Boston: G. K. Hall, 1989.

Atkinson, Brooks. "The Little Foxes," "Watch on the Rhine," "Another Part of the Forest," "Candide." In *Broadway.* New York: Macmillan, 1970. Reviews of original productions by influential *New York Times* critic.

Beebe, Lucius. "An Adult's Hour Is Miss Hellman's Next Effort" (1936). In *Conversations with Lillian Hellman,* edited by Jackson R. Bryer, 3–6. Jackson: University Press of Mississippi, 1986.

———. "Stage Asides: Miss Hellman Talks of her Latest Play, 'The Little Foxes'" (1939). In *Conversations with Lillian Hellman,* edited by Jackson R. Bryer, 7–10. Jackson: University Press of Mississippi, 1986.

Berger, Marilyn. "Profile: Lillian Hellman" (1979). In *Conversations with Lillian Hellman*, edited by Jackson R. Bryer, 232–73. Jackson: University Press of Mississippi, 1986. Fascinating, revealing, in-depth Hellman conversation with an intelligent interviewer.

Billson, Marcus K., and Sidonie A. Smith. "Lillian Hellman and the Strategy of the 'Other.'" In *Women's Autobiography: Essays in Crit-*

BIBLIOGRAPHY

icism, edited by Estelle C. Jelinek, 163–79. Bloomington: Indiana University Press, 1980. Perceptive introduction to the memoirs.

Broe, Mary Lynn. "Bohemia Bumps into Calvin: The Deception of Passivity in Lillian Hellman's Drama." In *Critical Essays on Lillian Hellman,* edited by Mark W. Estrin, 78–90. Boston: G. K. Hall, 1989.

Bromberg, Pamela S. "Establishing the Woman and Constructing a Narrative in Lillian Hellman's Memoirs." In *Critical Essays on Lillian Hellman,* edited by Mark W. Estrin, 115–28. Boston: G. K. Hall, 1989.

Clurman, Harold. *"The Autumn Garden."* In *On Directing.* New York: Macmillan, 1972.

———. "Lillian Hellman." In *Lies Like Truth.* New York: Macmillan, 1958. A distinguished critic and director comments on Hellman and her contemporaries.

Corrigan, Robert W. "Lillian Hellman." In *The Modern Theatre,* 1074. New York: Macmillan, 1964.

Culley, Margo, ed. "What a Piece of Work Is 'Woman'!" In *American Women's Autobiography: Fea(s)ts of Memory,* 3–31. Madison: University of Wisconsin Press, 1992.

dePue, Stephanie. "Lillian Hellman: She Never Turns Down an Adventure" (1975). In *Conversations with Lillian* Hellman, edited by Jackson R. Bryer, 184–91. Jackson: University Press of Mississippi, 1986.

Doudna, Christine. "A Still Unfinished Woman: A Conversation with Lillian Hellman." *Rolling Stone* 233 (24 February 1977): 52–57.

Drake, Sylvie. "Lillian Hellman as Herself" (1981). In *Conversations with Lillian Hellman,* edited by Jackson R. Bryer, 287–92. Jackson: University Press of Mississippi, 1986.

Falk, Richard A. *"Scoundrel Time:* Mobilizing the American Intelligentsia for the Cold War" (1977). In *Critical Essays on Lillian Hellman,* edited by Mark W. Estrin, 165–70. Boston: G. K. Hall, 1989.

Felheim, Marvin. "*The Autumn Garden:* Mechanics and Dialectics." In *Critical Essays on Lillian Hellman,* edited by Mark W. Estrin, 50–53. Boston: G. K. Hall, 1989.

Gardner, Fred. "An Interview with Lillian Hellman" (1968). In *Conversations with Lillian Hellman,* edited by Jackson R. Bryer, 107–23. Jackson: University Press of Mississippi, 1986.

Gassner, John. "Lillian Hellman: *The Autumn Garden.*" In *Theatre at the Crossroads.* New York: Holt, Rinehart, 1960. Important theater critic also analyzes her other plays.

Gellhorn, Martha. "On Apocryphism." In *Critical Essays on Lillian Hellman*, edited by Mark W. Estrin, 175–90. Boston: G. K. Hall, 1989. Writing by Stephen Spender, Hellman, and Ernest Hemingway attacked as untruthful.

Gilroy, Harry. "The Bigger the Lie." Introduction to *The Children's Hour: Acting Edition.* New York: Dramatists Play Service, 1953.

Glazer, Nathan. "An Answer to Lillian Hellman." *Commentary* 61 (19 June 1976): 36–39.

Goodman, Charlotte. "The Fox's Cubs: Lillian Hellman, Arthur Miller, and Tennessee Williams." In *Modern American Drama: The Female Canon,* edited by June Schlueter, 130–42. Rutherford, N.J.: Fairleigh Dickinson, 1990.

Gould, Jean. "Lillian Hellman." In *Modern American Playwrights,* 168–85. New York: Dodd, Mead, 1966.

Griffin, Alice. "Books—'Of a Different Feather: Lillian Hellman's *The Lark.*'" *Theatre Arts Magazine* 40 (May 1956): 8–10.

Harriman, Margaret Case. "Miss Lily of New Orleans: Lillian Hellman" (1941). In *Take Them up Tenderly.* New York: Knopf, 1944.

Heilman, Robert B. "The Southern Temper." In *Modern Southern Literature in Its Cultural Setting,* edited by Louis D. Rubin Jr. and Robert D. Jacobs, 48–59. Garden City, N.Y.: Doubleday, 1961. Places Hellman within the context of southern literature.

Hersey, John. "Lillian Hellman" (1976). In *Critical Essays on Lillian Hellman,* edited by Mark W. Estrin, 248–52. Boston: G. K. Hall, 1989.

Hollander, Anne, and John Phillips. "The Art of the Theater: Lillian Hellman, an Interview" (1965). In *Writers at Work: The Paris Review Interviews.* 3d ser. Edited by George Plimpton, 115–40. New York: Viking, 1967. Important, extensive interview with many revealing comments by Hellman.

Mason, Mary G. "The Other Voice: Autobiographies of Women Writers." In *Autobiography: Essays Theoretical and Critical,* edited by James Olney, 207–35. Princeton: Princeton University Press, 1980. Excellent historical and critical introduction.

Meehan, Thomas. "An Interview with Lillian Hellman" (1962). In *The Modern Theatre,* edited by Robert W. Corrigan, 1108–12. New York: Macmillan, 1964.

Miller, Arthur. "Why I Wrote *The Crucible.*" *The New Yorker* 72, no. 32 (21, 28 October 1996): 157–64.

Moyers, Bill. "Lillian Hellman" (1974). In *Conversations with Lillian Hellman,* edited by Jackson R. Bryer, 138–58. Jackson: University Press of Mississippi, 1986.

Patraka, Vivian M. "Lillian Hellman's *Watch on the Rhine:* Realism, Gender and Historical Crisis." *Modern Drama* 32, 1 (March 1989): 128–45.

Phillips, William. "What Happened in the Fifties." *Partisan Review* 43 (fall 1976): 337–40.

Poirier, Richard. "Introduction." In *Three.* Boston: Little, Brown, 1979. Outstanding critical analysis of first three memoirs.

Reed, Rex. "Lillian Hellman" (1975). In *Conversations with Lillian Hellman,* edited by Jackson R. Bryer, 179–83. Jackson: University Press of Mississippi, 1986.

Roughead, William. "Closed Doors." In *Bad Companions.* Edinburgh: W. Green, 1930. Hellman based *The Children's Hour* on this chapter.

Sherrill, Robert. "Wisdom and Its Price." *Nation* 222 (19 June 1976): 757–58.

Wiles, Timothy J. "Lillian Hellman's American Political Theater: The Thirties and Beyond." In *Critical Essays on Lillian Hellman,* edited by Mark W. Estrin, 90–112. Boston: G. K. Hall, 1989.

Zilboorg, Gregory, M.D. "Crime and Judgment." In *Mind, Medicine, and Man.* New York: Harcourt, Brace, 1943. Hellman's psychiatrist studies *Watch on the Rhine.*

Plays about Lillian Hellman

Feibleman, Peter. *Cakewalk.* An older but still feisty Lillian affectionately remembered by the author, her younger lover. New York: Dramatists Play Service, 1998.

Luce, William. *Lillian: A One-Woman Show.* Based on Hellman memoirs. New York: Dramatists Play Service, 1986.

Nelson, Richard. *Sensibility and Sense.* Feuding writers loosely based on Hellman and Mary McCarthy, 1989.

Movies about Lillian Hellman

Dash and Lilly. Directed by Kathy Bates, with Sam Shepard and Jody Davis, 1999.

Julia. Directed by Fred Zimmermann, with Jane Fonda as Hellman, 1977.

Academy Award, 115

Adams, Timothy Dow, 100–101, 126, 143, 145

Adler, Jacob, 13, 20, 35, 45, 79, 136, 137, 139, 140, 141, 142

Amato, Philip M., 33, 139

American, The, 57, 64

American Scholar, The, 126

Another Part of the Forest, 39–51; characters, 40–47; dialogue, 19–20, 47; family influence on, 9; movie, 121; plot, 47–48; reviews, 50–51; "satiric comedy," 21–22; setting, 39–40

Anouilh, Jean, 12

Are You Now or Have You Ever Been, 121

Arnold, Thurman, 122

Asquith, Margot, 65

Atkinson, Brooks, 7, 10, 13, 50, 136

Autumn Garden, The, 10–11, 76–88; characters, 76–88; Chekhov influence, 76, 88; Hammett help, 84; reviews, 11, 76; setting, 20, 77; structure, 76; theme, 80, 88; title, 76

Bad Companions, 4, 28

Beckett, Samuel, 131

Beebe, Lucius, 135

Bentley, Eric, 121

Berger, Marilyn, 136

Berkeley, Martin, 123

Bernstein, Leonard, 12–13

"Bethe," 110–11

Bibesco, Antoine, 65

Billson, Marcus K., 137

blacklist, 11–12, 119, 121, 123

Blechman, Burt, 14

Blessing, The, 123

Bloomgarten, Kermit, 121

Brandeis University, 15

Brecht, Bertolt, 63

Broe, Mary Lynn, 35, 139

Bromberg, Pamela, 101, 107, 142, 143

Buckley, William F., 126, 145

Cakewalk, 19, 121

Candide, Hellman's libretto, 12–13, 21; "Audition Precis," 21; "mistakes," 14; praised, 13

Cavett, Dick, 115

Central Intelligence Agency (CIA), 134

Channing, Stockard, 19, 56

Charles, Nick: *The Thin Man,* 3, 118

Charles, Nora: *The Thin Man,* 3

Chekhov, Anton: *The Autumn Garden,* 76; *The Cherry Orchard,* 12; *Letters,* 12, 25; *The Sea Gull,* 12; *Three Sisters,* 19, 94; *Toys in the Attic,* 89, 94

Children's Hour, The, 27–38; banned, 27; " the big lie," 4, 29–30, 37; characters, 29–35; dialogue, 4, 36; ending, 37; lesbianism, 27, 34–45; movies, 4, 37; production, 4; reviews, 16; revival, 4, 37–38, 121–22; source, 4, 28; success, 4, 27, 114; theme, 22, 28

Christians, Mady, 63

Clurman, Harold, 10, 20, 80, 137, 141, 142

Cohn, Harry, 121

Cohn, Roy, 119, 124

Columbia University, 16

Commentary, 126

Copland, Aaron, 8

Corrigan, Robert W., 22

"Cowan, Arthur W. A.," 110, 116–17
Crucible, The, 125

Davis, Bette, 74
Days to Come: contrasts, 22; plot, 5–6; theme, 6, 22
dePue, Stephaine, 135
dialogue, 23; *Another Part of the Forest,* 19; *The Children's Hour,* 4,
    36; *The Little Foxes,* 22, 60–61
Diary of Anne Frank, The, 75
Dick, Bernard F., 136
Dickens, Charles, 20
Doudna, Christine, 135
Downer, Alan, 96, 142
Drake, Sylvie, 138
Drama Critics' Circle, 13, 27, 64
Duffy, Martha, 18

Eliot, T. S., 3
Emerson, Ralph Waldo, 126
Estrin, Mark W., 18, 22, 63, 76, 125, 137, 139, 141, 144
Europeans, The, 7

Feibleman, Peter, 19, 121, 138
Felheim, Marvin, 88, 141, 142
female experience: imagery based on, 24–26, 125
Fonda, Jane, 115
Fortas, Abe, 120, 122
Four Plays: introduction to, 21, 22

Gardiner, Muriel, 115
Gardner, Fred, 138, 139

Gassner, John, 21, 23, 138

Gellhorn, Martha, 18, 100, 104, 115, 137, 144

Gershwin, Ira, 8

Gibbs, Wolcott, 63

Gilroy, Harry, 80, 138

Glass Key, The, 3

Glass Menagerie, The, 61

Glazer, Nathan, 126

Goldwyn, Samuel, 8

Goodman, Charlotte, 14, 61, 136

Gotti, Richard, 142

Griffin, Alice, 89, 136

Hammett, Dashiell: *The Autumn Garden,* 82, 84; "Bethe," 111; character and death, 116–18; dialogue, 124; drinking, 117; fame as writer, 3; HUAC, 120–21; meeting, 2; as mentor, 4; Pinkerton, 3, 120; relationship, 3, 103, 116–18; social commitment, 104–105, 120; *Toys in the Attic ,* 89; "Turtle," 117; *An Unfinished Woman,* 101, 108; *Watch on the Rhine* (screenplay), 74

Harriman, Margaret Case, 16, 64, 137, 139, 141

Harvard University, 15, 19

Heilman, Robert, 39, 139

"Helen," 107

Hellman family: aunts Hannah and Jenny, 93, 102, 128

Hellman, Lillian Florence: artistic theories and style, 19–26, 27; biographies of, 18; childhood and adolescence, 30, 102; early writing, 2; editor of Chekhov, 12; education, 1; employment, 1; farm, 7, 106, 123; father, 1; honorary degrees, 16; honors, 13, 16; HUAC, 11, 121–23; illnesses, 18; mother, 1; Southern influence, 23; Spanish civil war, 5; teaching, 15

Hellman, Max, 1, 93

Hemingway, Ernest, 115

Hersey, John, 1, 135
Hiller, Wendy, 99
Hollander, Anne, 135, 137, 144, 145
Holmin, Lorena, 142
honors and awards, 16
House Un-American Activities Committee (HUAC), 11, 16, 17, 119–24, 144
How Much?, 14
Howard, Maureen, 126
Hubbard family, 6, 7, 9–10, 39–62
Hunter College, 15
Huston, Walter, 9

Ibsen, Henrik, 35

James, Henry, 7, 20, 57
Jewish family, 2
Johnson, Diane, 144
Jonson, Ben, 39
"Julia," 18, 19, 104, 112–16

Karloff, Boris, 131
Kazan, Elia, 120–21
Klein, Carole, 142
Kober, Arthur, 2, 101, 103, 110
Korda, Alexander, 123
Kronenberger, Louis, 12

Lark, The, 12
Lederer, Katherine, 22, 89, 121, 142, 144
Leighton, Margaret, 99
Leverich, Lyle, 61, 137

Lillian, 121

Little Foxes, The, 6, 39–40, 51–62; characters, 52–60; dialogue, 22, 60–61; drafts of, 19; plot, 6; reviews, 7, 61–62; revival, 19, 97; "satiric comedy," 21–22; setting, 20; sources, 6; success, 7; themes, 6–7, 28, 51; title, 51

Liveright, Horace, 1, 103

Loy, Myrna, 3

Lucas, Paul, 74

Luce, William, 121

Martha's Vineyard, 129

Mason, Mary G., 109, 143

Maybe, 17–18, 103, 127–133; death as subject, 128–29; 131; imagery, 132; internal monologues, 132–33; style, 127, 131–32; subtitle, 130; symbolism, 129; tone, 133

McCarthy, Joseph, 9, 18, 22, 119, 124, 125

McCarthy, Mary, 18, 115

McCracken, Samuel, 116

Meehan, Thomas, 135, 138

Melby, John, 9

Mellen, Joan, 18

memoirs: characteristics of, 109–10; distinctive style, 15, 23–24, 100; dramatic effect, 17–18; innovations, 15. *See also individual book titles*

Metro-Goldwyn-Mayer, 2, 8, 103

Miller, Arthur, 14, 125, 136, 144

Miller, Theodore, 144

Mitford, Nancy , 123

Moers, Ellen, 23, 25, 138

Montserrat, 10

Morrell, Ottoline, 129

Mourning Becomes Electra, 42, 57

Moyers, Bill, 137
My Mother, My Father, and Me, 14

Nathan, George Jean, 16–17, 137
Nation, The, 126
National Book Award, 15, 100
National Institute of Arts and Letters, 15
National Review, 126
Neal, Patricia, 50
New Orleans: as birth place, 1; childhood in, 23, 102; as setting, 13
New Republic, The, 10, 104, 121
New York Post, 51, 76, 140
New York Times, 7, 50, 80, 126
New York University, 1
New Yorker, The, 2, 16, 63, 89, 141
Newhouse family, 1, 9–10, 39, 43, 47, 102
Newman, Robert P., 136
North Star, The, 8–9, 105

Odets, Clifford, 120, 124
Olauson, Judith, 139
Olney, James, 143
O'Neill, Eugene, 42, 57
Oresteia, 42, 57

Page, Geraldine, 99
Paris Review, 115
Parker, Dorothy, 107
Partisan Review, 126
Patraka, Vivian, 71, 141
Pentimento, 5, 9, 15, 17, 53, 102, 109–118; as autobiography, 109–10;
    "Julia" (movie version), 115; style, 109; title, 109

Phillips, John, 135, 137, 144, 145
Phillips, William, 126, 144
Piven, Shira, 19
Poirier, Richard, 15, 23, 135, 136, 138
Powell, William, 3
Pozner, Vladimir, 121
Preminger, Otto, 63

Rauh, Joseph, 120, 122
Redgrave, Vanessa, 115
Reed, Rex, 143
Rice, Vernon, 76
Robles, Emmanuel, 10
Rollyson, Carl, 18, 115–16, 136, 137, 138, 139, 141, 143, 144
Rome Daily American, 124
Roosevelt, Franklin D., 64
Roughead, William, 4, 28, 135
Royal National Theatre, 37–38
Rutgers University, 16

Saroyan, William, 8l9
Scanlon, Tom, 93, 142
Schine, David, 119, 124
Scoundrel Time, 11, 15, 17–18, 22, 24, 119–26; climate of fear, 119; HUAC hearing, 121–24; imagery, 125; lawyers, 120–21, 123; letter to HUAC, 121, 122–23; repercussions, 119, 123–24; reviews, 125–26; style, 124–25
Searching Wind, The, 8, 104
settings, 20
Sherill, Robert, 126, 145
Smith, Sidonie, 137
Song of Solomon, The, 51

Sophronia, 107
South: influence of, 23, 51, 102
Spacks, Patricia, 24, 138
Spanish civil war, 5, 63, 101, 104
Spender, Stephen, 115
Spengemann, William C., 143
Streetcar Named Desire, A, 45
Stuart, Ken, 19
symbols, 15, 107

Tavenner, Frank, 123
themes: courage, 12; family, 6, 23; female experience, 24–26l ; good
    and evil, 22; individual responsibility, 6, 23; money, 6, 23, 89, 90;
    morality, 51; self-knowledge, 89
These Three, 4
Thin Man, The, 3, 117
"This Is My Best," 104
Three, 81, 109, 114
Three Sisters, 19, 94
Time, 18
Toys in the Attic: aunts' influence, 93; characters, 13–14, 89–99;
    Chekhov influence, 19; Drama Critics' Award, 13; movie, 99; rela-
    tion to T. Williams, 13–14, 89; reviews, 89; setting, 20; structure,
    90; success, 14; themes, 89
Treisch, Manfred, 137, 139
Trollope, Anthony, 20
Tufts University, 16
Tynan, Kenneth, 89

Unfinished Woman, An, 5, 100–108; imagery, 107; Alice-Julia, 114;
    National Book Award, 15, 100; structure, 101; themes, 107; title,
    100–101; 108

University of California at Berkeley, 15
University of Texas: Humanities Research Center, 19

Volpone, 39
Voltaire: *Candide* libretto, 12, 21
von Stroheim, Eric, 9

Wadleigh High School, 1
Walcutt, Charles, 96, 142
Watch on the Rhine, 7, 63–75, 104; characters, 30, 68–72; inspiration
    for, 7, 57, 64; movie, 74; plot, 7, 64–66, 74–75; reviews, 7, 63–64;
    style, 67
Watts, Richard, 51
Weales, Gerald, 13, 136, 142
Wiles, Timothy J., 67, 141
Williams, Tennessee: influence on *Toys in the Attic,* 13–14, 89; influ-
    enced by *The Little Foxes,* 20, 61; *A Streetcar Named Desire,* 45
"Willy," 111–12
Wilson, Edmund, 13
women: position in society as seen in plays, 24–26, 28–29, 41, 44, 46,
    49–50, 54–56, 58–59, 60, 69–70, 71–72, 79, 92–94, 99
women's movement, 16
Wood, John S., 121, 123
Wright, William, 18

Yale University, 15, 16, 19